# Many Mansions
# Part II

# Why I Wrote This Book

I had several objectives in mind. I wanted, of course, first of all, to establish what evidence there was for reincarnation. Second, I wanted to integrate the information on reincarnation with modern psychology. Third, I wanted to integrate it with religion and especially Christianity. Fourth, I wanted to formulate some tentative laws of karma, or how reincarnation operated. Besides that, I had in mind to try to explain why human beings suffer—what the meaning is of human suffering.

So these were the five purposes I had in mind, and I wrote a book that was about 800 pages, which was about 300 or 400 pages too long. So the hardest part about it was to cut it. And the chapters that I cut out of this original manuscript, which became *Many Mansions*, later became *The World Within*. So *The World Within* really is an integral part of *Many Mansions*, although most people don't realize that. It carries to further lengths the themes that I had begun in *Many Mansions*, but it includes also the philosophy of balance, which I think was so essential a part of the Cayce approach.

Gina Cerminara
1975

# Many Mansions
## Part II

### Healing the Karma Within You

Gina Cerminara

**ARE PRESS**

ASSOCIATION FOR
RESEARCH AND
ENLIGHTENMENT

A.R.E. Press • Virginia Beach • Virginia

*"In this very body, six feet in length, with its sense-impressions and its thoughts and ideas, are the world, the origin of the world, and likewise the Way that leads to the ceasing thereof."*—BUDDHA

# Contents

Grateful acknowledgment is made to The Macmillan Company for permission to quote from the poem, "A Creed," by John Masefield.

# Preface

*Gina Cerminara, a psychologist, was one of a steady stream of individuals, profes-*sionals, and other seekers who came to Virginia Beach to study the work of the psychic Edgar Cayce. That stream continues today in a much larger way, due in part to the study, lecturing, and writing of Dr. Cerminara. She spent the years of 1946 and 1947 here in Virginia Beach collecting the material for her two books that form the basis for her study of the concept of reincarnation: *Many Mansions* and *The World Within*. Later she wrote another book on the same subject: *Many Lives, Many Loves*. These books have changed the lives of perhaps hundreds of thousands of people by introducing them to the concept of reincarnation—or perhaps to a more practical, applicable understanding of it.

Some of the influence of her books has been indirect. For example, I remember hearing Dr. Elisabeth Kübler-Ross say that it was her reading of Gina's books on reincarnation that stimulated her entry into the whole field of work with death and dying, and near-death experiences.

Dr. Kübler-Ross has, of course, helped countless people with her writing and study in this field.

In our travels together, I frequently introduced Gina as the person who had brought more people to a consideration of reincarnation than perhaps anyone else living. Many of us, including myself, have found this concept a helpful hypothesis in trying to understand our life and the lives of those around us.

Gina died in April, 1984. It was my privilege to lead a memorial service for her in Virginia Beach, where she lived from 1975 to 1983. At the service we learned about the Animal Assistance League of Virginia—an organization dedicated to the rescue, feeding, and adoption of unwanted and neglected animals—founded by Gina and two of her friends in 1976. We also heard from prison officials, nuns, priests, and other volunteers about the soup kitchens, state penitentiary, and many a poor neighborhood, both black and white, where Gina had gone to teach, serve food, or distribute clothing.

It is interesting to me that a frequent moral argument regarding reincarnation is that people will use it as an excuse to lead wasteful lives with the idea that they can do better "next time around." I have not found this to be the case with those I know who accept the concept of reincarnation, and this was not the case with Gina. She was a gifted writer and speaker who really lived by the principles of compassion and sanity about which she wrote and lectured.

The A.R.E. Press is proud to be able to reissue *The World Within*, now titled *Many Mansions Part II*. First published by William Sloane Associates of New York in 1957 as a companion to the well-known *Many Mansions*, it has been out of print for several years and therefore may not be known to many of those who have enjoyed *Many Mansions*.

We take particular pleasure in presenting this book to those of you who may be reading it for the first time. We feel certain it will be helpful in your study of reincarnation and the work of Edgar Cayce. This edition might be considered an opportunity for reacquaintance with an old friend and a tribute to Gina and her work.

Charles Thomas Cayce. Ph.D.
Executive director, A.R.E.

Introductory

# 1

# "But You Seem Too Intelligent . . . "

*"But you don't really believe in reincarnation, do you?"* the woman asked me, disapproval and incredulity sounding clearly in her college-bred voice.

I admitted to the lady that I really did.

There was a pause, then, in which I felt myself to be the object of careful scrutiny. "But you seem too intelligent a person to believe in such a thing!" she exclaimed at last.

It was an ambivalent compliment, if ever I heard one. But I was unable to resolve the seeming paradox in the lady's mind because of the press of other persons from the lecture audience about me.

And, as I thought about it later, it occurred to me that she had given expression to a widespread and typical point of view among the intellectuals of our time: to believe in reincarnation is, somehow, not quite intelligent.

At the same time, I felt a certain appreciation for the logic of her remark. I had had an experience myself, only a few years before, which gave me insight into her misgivings.

I was acquainted at that time with a man who probably had read most of the books on psychology and philosophy in the public library. He was easily one of the most learned persons I had ever known. One day I happened to meet him in the stacks of the Philosophy Room of the Milwaukee Public Library, and in the course of the long conversation that followed, he confided to me that he had recently designed a rocket ship for traveling to the moon.

This surprised me, but not too much: designing rocket ships to go to the moon may be an uncommon but certainly not a preposterous occupation at this stage of human history. But then he proceeded to tell me that he had just written a letter to the Coca-Cola Company, proposing that if they would finance the construction of his ship, and the voyage itself, he would, on arrival, erect a huge Coca-Cola sign completely across the diameter of the moon, so that the entire solar system would be reminded perpetually of "the pause that refreshes . . . "

At this point a look must have come into my eyes, though I struggled desperately to suppress it. "How can a man so intelligent in every other way," I was thinking, "be so daffy in this one?"

And so the remark of the woman from my lecture audience was quite understandable to me. Her reaction to me—and mine to my inventor friend—was the same feeling of mingled bafflement, sympathy, and suppressed hilarity that all persons experience who have dealings with the insane, some of whom can be completely rational for long periods of time and then all at once go off into a delusional system that defies comprehension.

Reincarnation, to most Europeans and Americans, is just such a delusional system—as lunatic a notion as the idea of a Coca-Cola sign across the entire diameter of the moon. It is regarded, if it is thought of at all, as a fantasy of the oriental mind to which in our country a motley crew of frustrated elderly women, dimwitted cultists, gullible Theosophists, and generally unintelligent crackpots have been attracted, like so many pathetic moths to an illusory flame.

Perhaps it is not too strange, though, that reincarnation should be in such intellectual disrepute. A materialistic philosophy is widespread among the intelligentsia, despite the fact that modern physics points the way to a non-materialistic view of the universe, and despite the fact that many leading physicists have, through the implications of their own science, been led away from materialism. But to the materialistic thinker—and this includes all Freudians, most psychologists, and all believers in Communist ideology—a "soul" is a ridiculous notion and even its survival after death, much less its evolution through repeated earth-experiences, quite unthinkable. (In fact, in Communist Russia it has been held a state crime to publish a book on reincarnation. Such a book obviously goes contrary to the very foundations of the dialectical materialism on which their system rests.)

A nine-year-old Hindu boy, writing an essay for his teacher on his favorite animal, the cat, touched on the very heart of one other major aspect of the matter. "The cat has four legs," he wrote, "one in each corner. He also has nine lives, which he does not use in Europe because of Christianity."

Like many other commentaries from children, this one is curiously significant. Christianity *has* made it difficult for anyone to make use of more than one lifetime—or even (let us admit it) to make use of his brains. In the sixth century at the Council of Constantinople, a group of Christian bishops formally outlawed by vote the teaching of reincarnation; it is still regarded as heresy by the Catholic Church. The Christian teaching on life, death, and the hereafter is strictly a one-throw game: our entire destiny in eternity is supposed to be determined by our behavior in this lifetime, no matter how short or how cruelly luckless it be.

But we are not allowed—as Christians, at least—to question this decision of the bishops or this perpetuation of a notion which has actually no shred of scientific evidence to support it, because the Christian faith—like other faiths—has for many centuries demanded of its followers an unquestioning conformity to its theology that admits of no search for truth elsewhere.

Paul set the pattern for rigidity and intolerance in these matters; in his letter to the Galatians he twice called down a curse on all those who should teach any gospel other than what he himself had taught. "But though we, or an angel from heaven, preach any other gospel unto you than that which we have preached unto you, let him be accursed," he wrote; and the attitude has persisted throughout all the intervening centuries.

A more mellow and tolerant attitude has gradually come to prevail in many places. Studies in comparative religion have led some people to realize that kindness and integrity and honor and even brotherly love are taught, with varying degrees of emphasis, by all great world faiths. The advance of science has compelled others to scrutinize Christian scriptures to discover whether or not they might in some respects have been symbolically rather than literally intended. Linguistic scholarship has awakened many to the fact that translations of the original documents on which Christianity is based have in hundreds of instances altered and distorted the original intention of scriptural writers. The recently discovered Dead Sea Scrolls may give us primary source material that can revolutionize some of our most deeply entrenched suppositions.

All these currents of thinking have led to the relaxation of religious orthodoxy in many quarters. But the majority of people are still religiously provincial; hence it is only natural for them to regard as heathen and false all explanations of human life and destiny alien to the pattern of their own traditional thinking.

Another reason for the scorn in which the idea of reincarnation is generally held by Europeans and Americans is that it is confused by most people with the idea of transmigration. This belief in the passage of the human soul to animal form after death is confused by casual observers with the more philosophic teaching of the evolution of human life through many successive human existences, which is the proper meaning of reincarnation. Whether or not a human soul can ever, under extraordinary circumstances, revert to animal form has been a matter of dispute among some reincarnationists; but the majority view, and the more psychologically credible one, is that, though a human soul can become progressively worse over a series of lifetimes, it cannot regress so far back as to enter animal form.

The theory of reincarnation is really the familiar scientific theory of evolution on a psychological and cosmic level. It affirms that each human soul is on a journey of return to its Source, which is God; that this journey of perfection cannot be accomplished in one short life span on earth; and that definite laws, rather than chance, operate to determine progressively the circumstances of every lifetime, or every stage of the journey. If more people were acquainted with the true position of reincarnationist thinkers, there would undoubtedly be less revulsion at the word.

Still another reason for the low esteem in which reincarnation is widely held by people in our portion of the globe is the general unawareness of the fact that many great Western intellects have thoroughly accepted the idea: Plato, Pythagoras, Virgil, Ovid, Giodano Bruno, Schelling, Leibnitz, Schopenhauer, Lessing, Fichte, Flammarion, Emerson, Walt Whitman, Carlyle, Edison, and Luther Burbank, to mention but a few.

The average well-educated person, exposed in school to the standard courses and the usual classics, is seldom made aware of the fact that many of the great thinkers and writers whose work he is studying were seriously convinced of the reality of reincarnation, and wrote as much and as explicitly concerning it as they felt advisable, considering the scorn in which they knew they might be held.

Most English and American college students, for example, have been required in a literature course to read some of the poetry of John Masefield, poet laureate of England. But how many of their college anthologies include Masefield's poem, "A Creed," in which he explicitly avows his belief in reincarnation? Masefield writes:

> I hold that when a person dies
> His soul returns again to earth;
> Arrayed in some new flesh disguise
> Another mother gives him birth.
> With sturdier limbs and brighter brain
> The old soul takes the roads again.

Or one can take a thoroughly brilliant course in the history of philosophy without once having it brought to one's attention that many of the major philosophers studied were fully persuaded of reincarnation. An entire course in Plato is frequently taught without a single reference being made to his distinct and explicit acceptance of the reincarnation idea—or, if reference is made thereto, it is dismissed as being a mere poetic fancy.

Students can get an A on their knowledge of Schopenhauer—and yet be totally ignorant of his revolutionary remark: namely, that if an Asiatic were to ask him for a definition of Europe, he would answer that it was that part of the world which was haunted by the incredible delusion that man's present birth was his first entrance into life . . .

The fact that many great writers and thinkers have accepted the theory of reincarnation—and written about it with varying degrees of frankness or caution—is, of course, not proof of the truth of the theory. But the fact that they *have* accepted it would, if better known, certainly lend more intellectual respectability to an idea, which is regarded by most people to be the crackpot notion of people from the lower brackets of intelligence.

Another reason for the indifference and the raised eyebrows with which reincarnation is regarded is that there would seem to be little scientific proof for the theory. At least, if there be such proof, the average man is completely unacquainted with it—as is, indeed, the average scientist. Individual scientists may have established evidence to their own private satisfaction, to be sure; but if so, they have not seen fit to publish their findings, well knowing that if they did so, they would probably be branded as mentally unbalanced by their colleagues. In short, no absolute, unequivocal, incontrovertible, laboratory-tested, *official* demonstration of the truth of reincarnation on a scientific basis has yet been made.

The temper of our age being what it is, it soon becomes apparent that this seeming absence of proof—or, at least, evidence—is a matter of cardinal importance.

Materialism, theological rigidity, ignorance, provincialism, indifference—all the obstructions which stand in the way of people giving an impartial consideration to so revolutionary and important a theory of human life as reincarnation—would of necessity crumble before the impact of *evidence*. Evidence, in short, is the new broom and the only broom that will sweep the horizon clean.

But even though official science—Science with a capital S—and the citadels of our universities have not presented us with such evidence, a strange thing has been taking place. Independently, and for the most part unknown to each other, persons of widely differing professional backgrounds have been stumbling upon data which in one way or another points to evidence for reincarnation.

Edgar Cayce, the great modern psychic, was perhaps the first of these stumblers in our century. As a young man of twenty-one he chanced to discover that he became clairvoyant when under hypnosis. He was able when in this state to diagnose and prescribe for people's diseases; and as a result of his sometimes seemingly fantastic counsel, hundreds of people were healed. The records of his forty years of activity in giving these "physical readings" were carefully kept and documented, and are available to any qualified investigator.

In 1925 he began to give indication (in what came to be called "life readings") that the causes for our present life situation and frequently even of our diseases are to be found in the past, in our previous incarnations on earth. He gave life readings for some 2,500 people; and these accounts not only proved to be psychologically accurate and therapeutically helpful, but also were frequently highly evidential as well.

Those who have read Thomas Sugrue's biography of Cayce, *There Is a River*, * or my own study, *Many Mansions*,† are familiar with the amazing records of this man's life work. *There Is a River* is the earlier book. It placed emphasis upon Cayce's life story and upon the medical clairvoyance that helped so many hundreds regain physical health. *Many Mansions* made more particular study of the life readings. It was: (1) a report on the evidence that substantiates these readings and tends to show that reincarnation may be a fact in nature; (2) an attempt to reduce to tenta-

---

*New York: Henry Holt 8: Co., Inc. 1943
†New York: William Sloane Associates, 1950

tive principles what seemed to be the operation of cosmic law in the human lives that Cayce analyzed; and (3) an attempt to integrate the thinking of modem psychology with the ancient teaching of reincarnation.

Both these books attracted moderate attention and have continued to be reprinted periodically. They appealed in large part to the metaphysical—occult public—people, that is, already interested in such unorthodox movements as Unity, Theosophy, Rosicrucianism, etc. However, they also drew considerable interest from laymen and professional people who had never heard of such movements. Evidence of this fact is to be found in the correspondence of these people either to the authors or to the Cayce Association, and in their appearing, many of them, at the Cayce headquarters in Virginia Beach, in quest of further information.

# 2

# Hey, Bridey Murphy!

*If there be anyone who does not know the story of Bridey Murphy,* a brief explana-*
tion may be in order.

Morey Bernstein, a prosperous young businessman of Pueblo, Colo-
rado, had for many years studied hypnotism as an avocation. He had
developed considerable skill in the art; in fact, he began to work with
various Pueblo doctors and helped a number of people to overcome
such conditions of psychosomatic origin as stuttering, migraine head-
aches, insomnia, excessive smoking, and hysterical paralysis.

In 1950, someone gave him copies of *There Is a River* and *Many Mansions*. He read them with intense interest until it became apparent that
the books dealt not only with healing through hypnosis, but also with
evidence for reincarnation. Skeptical almost to the point of outrage, he

---

*Morey Bernstein, *The Search for Bridey Murphy* (New York: Doubleday & Co., 1956) made a belligerent trip to the Cayce headquarters at Virginia Beach with the purpose of exposing the fraud at its source. Interviews with Hugh Lynn Cayce, Edgar Cayce's son, inspection of the documents, and a series of meetings with people who had had first-hand experiences with the readings caused a complete about-face in attitude. The Cayce material, he concluded, was honest at least, however preposterous it might seem.

Bernstein returned to Pueblo and began to experiment with the age-regression technique familiar to most psychologists; but this time he had the audacity to suggest to his subject that she regress *beyond* the time of her birth.

She did. She began to speak of a lifetime in Ireland in the nineteenth century, in which her name was Bridey Murphy, her first childhood memory being that of scratching the paint off her metal bed . . .

In this and succeeding sessions, Bridey Murphy's story unfolded coherently and consistently, the hypnotized woman frequently using words of which in her waking state she was ignorant but which were correct for the time and place. She used—accurately—"linen" for handkerchief; "flats" for a kind of cooking utensil; "cropping" to refer to farming; "ditch" to mean bury; and many other similar historically correct expressions not known to contemporary Americans or even, in some cases, to contemporary Irishmen. She also referred to places, events, coinage, crops, customs, and books, which Bernstein was later able to verify as being historically accurate.

A business matter took Bernstein to New York, and while there he brought his material to the attention of several major publishers. The editors of Doubleday felt as much enthusiasm as he did for the experiment and for its possibly important implications; and they contracted to publish a book on the subject.

Doubleday's plan was to have researchers in Ireland hunt up further confirmation of the hypnotized woman's story, Bernstein to have no part in the search in the interests of complete objectivity. The first part of the book was to be Bernstein's account of his experiment; the second part was to be the editors' independent check on the material. They proceeded to make inquiries by mail and by cable to Ireland, and some of the items not already established through American reference sources were confirmed in this way.

It soon became clear, however, that the task would be far more time-consuming and far less clear-cut than they had expected. But in the meantime, the machinery of publication had been set in motion, a publication deadline had been set, and already (due to a series of four articles on Bridey Murphy which had appeared serially in the *Denver Post* Sunday supplement and which had aroused phenomenal reader interest) they had close to ten thousand requests for, or inquiries about, the book. It is readily understandable, therefore, that the original plan was modified and that the book should have gone to press including whatever corroborating material they had been able to uncover to date, even though it was, admittedly, incomplete.

This haste in going to press was severely criticized in many quarters as being a thoroughly unscientific procedure on the part of Bernstein. Real scientists, it was pointed out, sometimes spend a lifetime in gathering data and becoming certain of their conclusions. The point is undoubtedly well taken; but at the same time it must not be lost sight of that (1) Bernstein acted in complete good faith, the agreement being that the publishers were to do the additional research in Ireland; and (2) Bernstein, a graduate in the field of commerce from the University of Pennsylvania, never had any pretensions of being a scientist. He did not conceive of himself as a Darwin or a Louis Pasteur. He was a businessman, anxious to get back to his business; *he frankly and openly avowed that his purpose in writing the book was merely to bring the strange results of his experiments to the attention of serious and qualified scientists.* "This is not an area," he writes in the last chapter of his book, "from which an airtight case should be expected. The whole issue, rather, is whether the principles involved here merit more intensive consideration."

In the light of the forthcoming devastating, if biased, attacks on the Bridey Murphy story, it might have been well if the publishers had waited until the case had been investigated more thoroughly. But in view of what Bernstein's major purpose was, it probably doesn't much matter. Not only did the Bridey Murphy case come to the attention of serious scientists—it came to the attention of everybody else in the range of printer's ink, as well.

Within two weeks of the book's publication date it had reached best-seller lists. Bookstores were hard put to keep up with the demand. In five months it went through ten printings, amounting to 205,500 copies. Fifty-one newspapers throughout the country serialized the book; some of them repeated the series twice because of the unprecedented demand for back copies. Paramount Pictures bought the movie rights for documentary treatment. Translations were arranged for in Holland, France, Italy, Denmark, Sweden, Spain, and Finland. An incident that rather epitomized the extravagance of public excitement was the case of a man in Chicago who walked into Kroch's and Brentano's bookstore and bought the entire window display: 166 copies of *The Search for Bridey Murphy*.

People began giving Come-as-You-Were costume parties; a Houston, Texas, cocktail lounge was serving a Reincarnation Cocktail; night club performers were putting on burlesque age-regression experiments; four songs in popular vein appeared: "The Love of Bridey Murphy"; "The Ballad of Bridey Murphy"; a burlesque version by Stan Freeberg, "The Quest for Bridey Hammerschlagen"; and one in the prevailing mode of "Rock and Roll." (First line: "Bridey Murphy did the rock and roll a hundred years ago. HEY, Bridey Murphy!. . .")

At the same time, Bridey became the subject of endless quips and jokes. People told the story of a man who read about Bridey Murphy and then changed his will: he left everything to himself . . . They also told about a man who regressed his wife to the seventeenth century and left her there . . . A cartoonist showed two women in a supermarket; one was angrily telling the other: "So then he started calling me Bridey Murphy. Said nobody could learn to cook as badly as I do in just one lifetime." It is to be wondered at, perhaps, that no enterprising merchant came out with a Bridey Murphy Cat Food—Good for Nine Lives. . . .

In short, the Bridey Murphy story had become a public craze comparable, as *Life* magazine pointed out, to the great crazes for the ouija board, mahjong, Technocracy, Davy Crockett, and other fads that from time to time take hold of the public imagination. Morey Bernstein had become the Liberace, as it were, of the reincarnation world.

But though many people deplored the levity and flippancy with which Bridey was discussed, and others dismissed the whole thing as utter nonsense or as "sensationalism," thousands of persons were stimulated to serious thought and serious conversation as well. Booksellers noted a distinct upswing in the sales of books relating to hypnosis and reincarnation. Discussions of Bridey Murphy could be heard and overheard in buses, breweries, offices, smoking cars, restaurants, airplanes, garages, and barbershops; on street corners and college campuses; in California and in Ireland; in rooming houses and at dinner parties. Reincarnation was being earnestly, and sometimes hotly, argued by persons, some of whom had never heard the word before, some of whom had always secretly believed in it but never dared say so, and some of whom had long and openly believed in it but never had so much ammunition as the Bridey Murphy story now seemed to provide them.

Not only was the public reading about Bridey Murphy, singing about her, making jokes in her name, and discussing her with deadly earnestness; they were also experimenting, themselves, with hypnotic age-regressions.

All over the country people were telling other people, in slow rhythmic command, to go "deeper and deeper, deeper and deeper"; and all over the country, while tape-recording spools slowly turned, people were falling into what seemed to be past lives as Civil War soldiers, Indo-Chinese dancing girls, French courtesans, or Spanish peasants. A skeptical reporter on the *Los Angeles Mirror-News*, John Grover by name, submitted to an age-regression experiment—and, to his own amazement, came up as a German cobbler of fourteenth-century Hamburg, even speaking a few words of German, a language which he says he does not know in his normal state. One of the most curious things about the experiment, in Grover's opinion, was his use of the word *pud* for a measure of weight, which research disclosed was a Russian weight of the period, and which might well have been known to tradesmen in European seaports. Another aspect of the experiment, which Grover said he found impressive was his very distinct sensation of the odor of tidewater mud in the Elbe River as he was presumably reliving the

Hamburg life. Grover's experience was typical. Not only believers but skeptics, too, found themselves thinking seriously about things and, what is more, experiencing things, that they had never been aware of before.

This extraordinary frenzy of public interest is in itself an interesting psychological phenomenon. It can be understood perhaps as a manifestation, first, of the perennial interest in anything that concerns life after death; second, of the almost universal fascination that hypnosis wields over people's imaginations; third, of the extraordinary uncertainty of our times, which leads to an intensified desire for cosmic certainties; and fourth, of the tenderized state, so to speak, of the public mind, so stunned by incredibles—such as H–bombs, flying saucers, supersonic speeds, magic–eye doors, radar–controlled traffic, television, interplanetary rockets, man–made satellites—that an anything–is–possible attitude has become more and more prevalent in the past two decades.

From the very beginning, of course, the Bridey Murphy story was attacked on all sides. Though very few people seemed to call in question Mr. Bernstein's honesty and sincerity in the matter (it was widely recognized that as a prospering businessman he had little to gain and much to lose by perpetrating a hoax), many regarded him as a "naive," "inexpert," and "wide–eyed" amateur who was playing with things he knew little or nothing about, and "breathlessly" relating them to his intellectual superiors. But the story itself was vigorously challenged, and this from two widely differing vantage points: that of religion, and that of science.

Some theologians angrily called it "the work of devils" or "of Satan"; many religiously orthodox people were incensed because it went, they said, contrary to the teachings of the Bible; others regarded it with complacent finality as something they had known about for a long time and naturally dismissed as heresy. On the scientific front, psychiatrists attacked the story on the grounds that (1) a hypnotized subject is suggestible, and, desiring to please the operator, will produce what is expected of him; (2) mere coincidence accounted for the facts verified in

Ireland; the other details were nothing more than subconscious memories of things heard in childhood.

Dr. Schneck (former President of the Society for Clinical and Experimental Hypnosis) and Dr. Lewis Wolberg (Medical Director of New York's Postgraduate Center for Psychotherapy) stated that: "The attempt to check the story's truth in Ireland was roundabout. There was a more direct way. That was simply going to the woman's childhood and development . . . That would tell us more than trying to check old newspapers in Ireland."

In February, 1956, William Barker (the reporter whose four-installment account of Bridey had been published in the *Denver Post* months before) went to Ireland to attempt to confirm some as yet unconfirmed details. Bernstein himself felt that the long-distance research done by the publishers was far from satisfactory; the *Denver Post* editors did also, and they decided to sponsor Barker on a three-week trip to Ireland. Barker's search—which he wrote up later for the *Denver Post* under the title "The Truth About Bridey Murphy"—was interesting but inconclusive. Many of the statistical records, which he consulted were incomplete; some had been destroyed; some were unavailable. The Irish were courteous and helpful, but because of their deep religious convictions they were for the most part incapable of believing that there could be any truth in the Bridey Murphy story. Their first reaction was almost invariably negative and skeptical with regard to anything that seemed likely to confirm Bridey's actual existence, though subsequent research frequently proved their very absolute opinions to have been wrong. Despite these two not inconsiderable difficulties, Barker *was* able to confirm some items of Bridey's account, though many others he was not.

In March, a magazine with a large national circulation gave a curiously distorted picture of Barker's report. For example, this magazine stated that with regard to Bridey's referral to "The Sorrows of Deirdre," the name of Deirdre in a book title *did not appear anywhere before 1905.* But Barker had found—and expressly so stated—a listing of a paperback volume, printed in both English and Gaelic, of "The Sorrows of Deirdre" as early as 1808. The magazine reported flatly that iron bedsteads were not used in Ireland before 1850, so Bridey obviously could not have scratched the paint off one in her childhood; but Barker had found many indications (including references in the Encyclopaedia Britannica and the notebooks of Thackeray) that they *were* used early in the century. This kind of misrepresentation ran through the magazine's report, and did much to discredit the story in public eyes.

However, in May of the same year, the most devastating attack of all appeared. It was called "Bridey Murphy a Mystery No Longer," and it ran daily in serialized form in the *Chicago American*.

A Reverend Wally White of the Chicago Gospel Tabernacle learned that Bernstein's subject—to whom the name Ruth Simmons had been given to protect her identity—had once been a student in the Sunday School of his church. Taking a leaf from the psychiatrists' notebook, he felt that a thorough study of Ruth Simmons' childhood would disclose that all the so-called Bridey Murphy memories were nothing else than memories of her present-life childhood, transposed. He frankly stated that his purpose was to demolish the Bridey story because it went so dangerously contrary to Christian orthodoxy.

Together with reporters from the *Chicago American*, Mr. White succeeded in demonstrating, he claimed, that (1) as a child, Ruth Simmons had scratched the paint off her metal bed; (2) she had a friend and neighbor whom she affectionately called "Uncle Plazz"; (3) she had excelled in dramatics, was an excellent mimic, and had frequently recited monologues in Irish brogue; (4) she had often danced Irish jigs; (5) there was a woman still living in Chicago named Bridey Murphy Corkell who had been a neighbor of Ruth Simmons and with whose children Ruth Simmons played as a child. (This last circumstance was announced with particular triumph. The picture of Mrs. Corkell was printed in many publications with captions such as "Bridey Murphy Found at Last—She Was in Chicago All the Time.")

All of these details, then, became "paraphrased," as Mr. White put it, into the imaginary life of Bridey Murphy who, as readers of the book will recall, scratched the paint off her much disputed metal bed in Ireland; had an Uncle Plazz; spoke in authentic Irish brogue; and danced a morning jig—all under hypnosis.

In the eyes of many people, the case was now closed. Ministers all over the country breathed sighs of righteous relief. God was no longer mocked; purgatory, hell, resurrection, and salvation were still safely in place where they ought to be. Psychiatrists were intensely pleased. "It is wonderful!" exclaimed one New York psychiatrist, in comment on the investigation, ". . . exactly what I hoped someone would do." Dr. Lewis Wolberg referred to it as "an invaluable service in making known the specific events of Ruth Simmons' life which she wove together to form her reincarnation fantasy." Bridey Murphy's ghost—to use a phrase popular in the tabloids—had now been laid. In psychiatric and ministerial circles, a triumphant I–told–you–so spirit pervaded the atmosphere, and there was a pleasant sense of business as usual.

But actually, the sighs of relief and the I–told–you–so's were premature. For one thing, Ruth Simmons herself, both privately and in a published interview with *Denver Post* reporters, disclaimed the truth of many of the *Chicago American's* "findings." According to Ruth herself, for example, she never knew at any time in her life a person whom she called "Uncle Plazz." She did not remember any incident of having scratched paint off her bed as a child. She also disclaimed (as did her childhood elocution teacher in Chicago when interviewed by *Denver Post* reporters) that she had any gift for mimicry; she said that the only dances she ever did in childhood were the Charleston and the Black Bottom—and never any Irish jigs. She remembered Mrs. Corkell, *but she never knew that her first name was Bridey or her maiden name, Murphy.* It is unlikely, in fact, that any child should know the first name or maiden name of the mothers of his playmates. Even adults living in a big city like Chicago do not usually know the first and maiden names of their next–door neighbors.

It would almost seem, then, that some of the details of this story were invented from whole cloth; certainly most of the so–called parallels of the two lives were strained to the breaking point. To explain away Bridey's death from a fall down the steps, for example, on the grounds that her present–life sister had a fall down the steps as a young child, is to explain away nothing at all. Moreover, parallels could occur in any two lifetimes and still not disprove the fact that an earlier event did occur.

It is not at all unlikely that, mixed with valid recollections of nine-teenth-century Ireland, an occasional childhood memory from twenti-eth-century Chicago could have interposed itself. A hypnotized subject, as William Barker points out, is not under oath and he does not become omniscient; he does not remember everything with perfect accuracy and what he does remember can be drawn from various levels of time in the memory.

But most important of all is the fact—studiously overlooked by the writers of this superficial newspaper expose—that no matter how many Irish comic monologues Ruth may have recited as a child, Irish comic monologues do not contain detailed historical information, such as the fact that there was a greengrocer named John Carrigan and a foodstuff dealer named Farr in nineteenth-century Belfast; that there were two tiny places named Doby and Bailie's Cross, not listed on any maps any-where but confirmed in Ireland by an Irish Catholic priest and an Irish farmer as having actually existed in County Cavan; that there was a coin called a "tuppance" in Ireland in that period (contrary to the first opinion of "experts" who had absolutely disclaimed it until careful search proved them wrong); and many other details which were un-questionably confirmed in Ireland.

It may be years before all the evidence in the Bridey Murphy case has been accumulated and thoroughly examined; there must be an honest and careful sifting of what may be childhood subconscious memories from what may be genuine past-life recalls; and it must be done, not by people who have an admitted bias and religious compul-sion to disprove Bridey's story, but by persons who are capable of real objectivity in the matter. It would be interesting, also, and perhaps very instructive, if Ruth Simmons would consent to be hypnotized by an-other hypnotist, and regressed to another past life in another era—one which had no correspondences to her present-life exposure to Irish influences.

But even had it been possible—and, despite the anxious, hasty, and superficial flurry of critics it has not been—to demolish the Bridey Murphy evidence completely, the court of examinations *still* could not adjourn. There is too much evidence already in existence elsewhere.

And there is fresh evidence, brought to light since Bridey Murphy, with corroborative detail in some cases even more difficult to dispose of than Bridey's. The case for reincarnation does *not* stand or fall merely on the strength of Bridey Murphy—any more than the case for evolution stood or fell on the strength of the famous Tennessee trial.

# 3

# Other Brideys, Other Bernsteins

*To assume, a priori, that reincarnation must be false is an unscientific attitude—as* unscientific as to assume that the world *must* be flat because it appears so to our senses. Yet many scientists and "experts" called in on forums and panel discussions of the Bridey Murphy case have taken this attitude, and have tried to clip all the facts of the case to fit the Procrustean bed of their basic unwarranted assumption. "None but very hasty thinkers," wrote Professor Thomas Henry Huxley in *Evolution and Ethics,** "will reject reincarnation on the grounds of inherent absurdity."

Quite apart from the logical and philosophical reasonability of the idea as argued by many thinkers in both the East and the West, there already exist three major types of evidence that support its validity. These may be classified as follows: (1) Cases of spontaneous memory of

---

*New York: D. Appleton & Co.

a past life; (2) Cases of regression induced by hypnosis, free association, or other psychological techniques; (3) Clairvoyance or mediumship which sets forth past-life causes for present-life situations, accompanied by some subjective or objective corroborations.

Of the spontaneous cases, the one of Shanti Devi is perhaps the best authenticated and the most airtight example on record.

As every reader of *The Search for Bridey Murphy* will remember, this is the case of a small girl in Delhi, India, named Shanti Devi. She kept prattling about her former life in Muttra, India, with so much detail and so much insistence that her parents, on the advice of the local schoolmaster, finally decided to take her to Muttra. In the presence of substantial witnesses (including a nationalist leader, a well-known lawyer, and the editor of a great Indian newspaper), and under strictest test conditions, the child recognized her previous husband, her former brother, and the young son at whose birth, in the previous life, she had died. She also spoke to her husband of many intimate details of their life together (admitted by him to be accurate), and she located a hiding place for money, in the house where she had formerly lived.

There are many other similar (though for the most part less complete) cases of spontaneous memory that have been reported and, in one way or another, validated. Travelers in the Orient hear of them more frequently, perhaps, than we do in the Occident; but even among us, there are innumerable instances which have been recorded, and which would be very difficult to account for adequately on any hypothesis other than reincarnation.

Cases such as these cannot be disposed of with the standard objections made to hypnotic material (such as: intensified imagination; desire to please the hypnotist; or "paraphrased" unconscious material from childhood) for the simple reason that they did not take place under hypnosis.

Moreover, they cannot be dismissed by attributing them, as have some critics of reincarnation, to a "hereditary memory factor," by which is meant "genes which carry memories from one generation to the next, just as physical traits are carried from one generation to the next." In the case of Shanti Devi, for example, it obviously could *not* have been a hereditary memory; she was born to an entirely different family, hundreds of miles away from the family she remembered being a part of in the very recent previous life. (She was reborn about a year after her previous death.) Besides, the "hereditary memory factor" theory is an unproved one that would be just as difficult to prove, and probably more so, than the reincarnation theory itself.

These cases of spontaneous memory are usually looked at by psychologists—if at all—with unseeing eyes; or, if their existence is actually acknowledged, they are shrugged off as being hearsay stories and old wives' tales or, at best, as being interesting, but not susceptible to control conditions. Sometimes they are labeled *deja vu* experiences—a French term meaning "already seen"—and for the most part, explanations of *deja vu* are not only inadequate to the facts, but also elaborately couched in what can best be called psychological double talk.

But there are other sources of evidence which are *not* hearsay or *deja vu* and which were obtained under careful controls. These are systematic bodies of case—history material, which though independently arrived at, parallel each other and the Bridey Murphy story. And this material cannot be easily dismissed by anyone who has enough intellectual curiosity or enough scientific alertness to recognize that any unexplained fact, however preposterous, may lead to the discovery of something important.

In 1950, Blanche Baker of San Francisco, a Ph.D., M.D., and psychiatrist, read *Many Mansions*. She felt that the hypothesis of reincarnation was sufficiently reasonable to warrant further investigation. If the Cayce material were true, she reasoned, then the memories of past lives should be buried at deep levels of the unconscious and might conceivably be available to therapeutic dredging. Her motivation was not so much that of proving or disproving the reincarnation hypothesis, as it was that of answering to her own satisfaction the questions: Can past-life memories be obtained? And if so, can they release patients from psychosomatic illness or psychological distress?

Though recognizing the value of hypnosis as a research tool, she felt that other techniques might be ultimately more fruitful in a therapeutic situation. She decided to use a modification of Freud's method of free association, and she began to find in sessions on the analytical couch that most of her patients—though she had given them *no* suggestion that they were to go into "past lives"—began seeing themselves in strange, dramatic scenes of violence or death or curious interpersonal relations. This happened even to people of orthodox religious background who had never heard of reincarnation, and who sometimes found it necessary to say, "It seems as if I must have lived somewhere before." Like John Grover, the *Los Angeles Mirror-News* reporter who experienced a vivid smell of the mud on the Elbe River flats, these people had vivid sensations of smell and taste and touch as well as visual images, and not only physical pain but emotional anguish was often acutely experienced.

These could well have been dismissed as fantasy dramatizations, were it not for the fact that so much of the detail given by the patients with regard to past historical epochs was found, on checking, to be historically accurate. This included such matters as climate, historical events, costume, custom, names, and dates.

One of the doctor's patients, a woman of Scotch–English–American ancestry, born in Utah and of a very meagre educational background, has brought through a total of forty–seven lives (twenty–three as a man, twenty–four as a woman); literally hundreds of details from these lives have been verified in historical reference books. In one session, witnessed by the writer, she relived with great vividness an experience as a messenger on the island of Malta in the year 870 A.D. Speaking with a male voice, she said she was a Greek by the name of Icon; she was walking over very rocky terrain, bringing a message, written on her back, to the Arabs from one of the ruling families. She expressed concern that the message would cause the loss of many lives; indicated that the people of the island were a mixed race; that the climate was mild and never cold, and that there was running water on the island. When the message was delivered, the Arabs proceeded to brand the words off the messenger's back so that no trace of it would remain . . . The branding scene was relived with considerable anguish and lifelike contortions on the couch.

But the point is that the Encyclopaedia Britannica later yielded the information that Malta *is* a rocky island with perennially flowing streams; that it was governed at the time by several noble families and populated by a mixed race composed of Normans, Spanish, and Italians; that the climate is temperate but never cold; that in the year 870 A.D. there was an Arab invasion and that 3,000 Greeks were massacred. All these facts were unknown to both Dr. Baker and the subject.

In still another memory, this same woman mentioned being helped by a woman doctor named Dr. Marie Boivin in Paris in 1820. Once again the existence of this obscure woman physician was totally unknown to both Dr. Baker and the subject; later they found a brief biography of her in *A History of Women in Medicine* by Kate Campbell Hurd-Mead, M.D.,* in which it was indicated that Dr. Marie Boivin had practiced medicine in Paris in exactly the period referred to.

This sort of thing *cannot* be cheaply dismissed as a paraphrased childhood memory; and similar cases occur by the hundreds in Dr. Baker's work with many different patients, numerous examples of which have been carefully preserved by tape recording. "Coincidence" is the stock explanation offered by skeptics for these occurrences; but this explanation is, at best, inadequate, in view of the frequency with which they occur. The only alternate explanation possible (the integrity of the parties involved being beyond reproach) would be that independent acts of telepathy or clairvoyance had occurred each time such verifiable details appear; but under the circumstances, this is a much more farfetched explanation, and accounts for less of the facts, than reincarnation itself.

It is important to note that Dr. Baker does not use hypnosis nor does she ask many leading questions. It is also important to note that her patients experience great therapeutic benefits as a result of these regressions. Worthy of note, also, is the fact that frequently some physical difficulty, as for example a sore throat, an injured elbow, or a painful back is tied in with the past-life tragedy that is revived under therapy. The woman whose case is cited above, for example, had felt great pain in her lower back for twenty-four hours before she relived the branding scene of Malta; the backache disappeared after the release of the memory.

---

*Middletown, Conn.: Haddam Press, 1938

At the same time, other investigators have been working along similar lines, quite independently of each other and sometimes with no knowledge of the Cayce material.*

Any number of hypnotists, both of professional and amateur standing, have also reported the emergence of past-life recalls in hypnotic sessions. Outstanding among these is professional psychologist and hypnotist Emile Franchel, originally of London, England, and now of Van Nuys, California, who in 1956–57 conducted a popular Los Angeles television show called "Adventures in Hypnotism." On these programs, Mr. Franchel demonstrated hypnosis in its many forms, and he was the first person ever to conduct past-life and other regression experiments before television cameras.

Mr. Franchel prefers to consider himself a skeptic on the question of reincarnation, and stated in an interview with the author that he would like to dismiss the whole thing as (in his own words) "hogwash." He maintains that much of the apparent "past-life" recall obtained under hypnosis is due principally to the asking of leading questions by the experimenting hypnotist, who—either as a devout believer in reincarnation is unwittingly desirous of proving a case for it—or, as a showman, is interested simply in intriguing an audience.

---

*Editor's footnote: Interested readers may wish to study further some additional material. One such work is an article written by Michael Dennis, Ph.D., a former research associate of Dr. Ian Stevenson's, which appears in two parts in *The A.R.E. Journal* (January and March, 1984, Volume XIX, Numbers 1 and 2; published by the Association for Research and Enlightenment, Inc.). Entitled "The Scientific Evidence for Reincarnation: A Summary of Three of Ian Stevenson's Best New Cases and a Proposal for Future Research," the article presents three case summaries of the reincarnation type as well as an outline of the social science context for scientific investigation into past lives and concludes with a proposal for future reincarnation research.

An interview with Ian Stevenson, M.D., director of the Division of Parapsychology at the University of Virginia and author of *Twenty Cases Suggestive of Reincarnation* (Charlottesville: University of Virginia, 1974; 2nd ed., rev. and enl.), appears in two parts in the September/October and November/ December, 1984, issues of *Venture Inward* (Volume I, Numbers I and 2), published by the A.R.E.

In other cases, the apparent regression to a past life can be accounted for, Mr. Franchel says, as "genetic memory," the apparent past lives merely being, in some measure, the experience of an ancestor in the subject's hereditary stream.

But—Mr. Franchel admits—one per cent of the cases can *not* be accounted for in these ways, and therefore may be accountable by the reincarnation hypothesis; and there are a number of cases in his own files which he acknowledges as belonging to this uncomfortable one per cent.

One of these cases is that of Beverly Richardson, a young lady of Northridge, California (born in the state of Montana) who, in pre–birth age–regression experiments before television cameras, went back to a very recent apparent past life in a small town named Corning, Ohio. She declared, under hypnosis, that she was forty years old in 1898 and that her name was Mrs. Jean MacDonald. She gave a number of details concerning the town and her life there, and the descriptions of the town at least were subsequently confirmed in the main by two elderly people—each independent of the other—who viewed the television show and, as old–time residents of Corning, Ohio, remembered the town as the age–regressed subject described it.

In an effort to double check her veracity, Mr. Franchel and the producers of the television show contacted the Zanesville Publishing Company of Zanesville, Ohio (the nearest large town to Corning) and requested them to send some large photographs of various street scenes and locales in Corning. The publishing company sent pictures showing:

1) a rear view of the subject's former house (the address of which she had given under hypnosis);

2) the stream that ran nearby;

3) the building which had previously housed the town newspaper (but which had been used for many other businesses since and bore no distinguishing sign);

4) the Corning railway depot;

5) the old Kincaid stables (now a garage);

6) Main Street of Corning.

When the subject was again in the hypnotic state and again regressed, Mr. Franchel attempted an experiment that had, up to then, been seen only by a very few professional experimenters. He asked the subject to open her eyes and *to remain the regressed personality*. He then showed her the pictures. Without ever having seen them before, she correctly recognized and identified the contents of each of the pictures!

With regard to (1) her previous house, she questioned the presence of a garage, which had been built lately on the property. She also remarked on the fact that this was a *rear* view of the house—which was correct, because of street changes made since 1898, though to a casual observer this might not have been obvious.

With regard to pictures (3) and (6), she correctly identified the newspaper building and the street, but was puzzled by the presence of automobiles. "What are these things?" she asked Mr. Franchel, pointing to the cars. Taken aback, he said quickly, "Carriages. A new kind of carriage." "But where are the horses?" she persisted. With regard to picture (5) she recognized the back part of the building, which at one time had housed the stables in which her husband presumably had worked, but was puzzled by the large front addition which had been constructed by the garage now occupying the structure.

Some of the unique features of this unusual case are: 1) the fact that it was presented, unrehearsed, on television before a very large television audience; 2) the fact that Beverly Richardson was born in the state of Montana, of parents who had never been to Corning, Ohio, and no trace of a connection could be found with Corning on the part of either herself or her parents; 3) the fact that the places and people described were within the living memory of persons, strangers to the subject, who later confirmed her account; 4) the fact that the subject correctly identified pictures placed before her of scenes which she could not have ever seen in her present lifetime, and was aware of changes made from that epoch to the present.

Another interesting and unusual case is to be found in the files of consulting psychologist Dr. Paul Hughes of Montebello, California. This is the case of a young woman who, when pre–birth age–regressed, went back to a life in Egypt in which she had been buried alive by her father.

About fifty sessions brought out the story in great detail; but the most interesting feature of the case was that she several times spoke in what seemed to be the language of the period.*

Dr. Hughes called in a native-born Egyptian, Mr. Abdel Salam Moussa (M.A., 1957, University of Southern California), who was acting at the time as technical adviser to several Hollywood studios on pictures with an Egyptian setting, and who was also working toward his Ph.D. degree. Mr. Moussa reported to Dr. Hughes and to the present writer that many of the words which the young woman used were unintelligible to him, but that many others were unmistakably words of the ancient Coptic. She also answered him accurately with regard to various ancient Egyptian customs, known to him and unknown to herself and Dr. Hughes (or, indeed, to any average contemporary American).

In the spring of 1958 newspapers throughout the United States carried the story of a case which paralleled the Bridey Murphy story, but which gave promise of surpassing it in evidential strength.* This was the case of a 29-year-old housewife, Mrs. Norbert Williams of Indianapolis, Indiana, who, in a regression experiment with her hypnotist uncle, Richard E. Cook, recounted a lifetime as a confederate soldier named Jean Donaldson.

Though in her conscious state she speaks as a cultured Middle Westerner, under hypnosis Mrs. Williams used the unmistakable vocabulary and drawl of a southern farm boy; and in seven regression sessions she gave detailed information concerning various Civil War battles in one of which young Donaldson lost his life.

According to the hypnotic account, Donaldson was born March 4, 1841, on a farm near Shreveport, Louisiana. In 1862 he joined the Confederate Army, and at the Battle of Shiloh he saw his best friend killed.

---

*For an interesting parallel case of the use of ancient Egyptian by a contemporary person, see Frederic Herbert Wood, *This Egyptian Miracle* (2nd edition; London; John Maurice Watkins, 1955).

*One of the most complete coverages of the story can be found in the *Shreveport Magazine* (published by the Shreveport Chamber of Commerce) for May, 1958.

Soon after, he lost his own right eye. He was made a corporal and fought another two years. Finally at Nashville (or possibly elsewhere; this detail is not clear) he received a fatal wound in his side and died.

These are the broad outlines of the story, though it included many names of people, places, streets, and other incidental details. Through the combined efforts of a number of researchers, certain confirmations have been obtained. For example:

1) It has been established that a Donaldson family *did* live on a farm southwest of Shreveport before the Civil War, and that 2) Jean Donaldson *did* exist. (In this respect at least the case has greater cogency than the Bridey Murphy case, inasmuch as no such person as Bridey was ever really found in Ireland.) 3) It was stated in the regression that a man named Duncan was a neighbor of the Donaldsons. A December 5, 1868, deed in the courthouse showed that a James Duncan owned a piece of property 2½ miles south of what was then Shreveport. 4) There *was* a *Shreveport Gazette* published in 1860, confirming the subject's account. 5) An official report regarding militia units mustered in Louisiana in 1860 included the name of Jean Donaldson in the 2nd division. 6) Congressional records show Donaldson's enlistment. 7) As stated in the regression, there really *was* a Watter Street in early Shreveport.

There were several other confirmations and near-confirmations of this nature, the lack of adequate historical records making it impossible to check every statement made by the subject. And yet even such skimpy confirmations as these are still extraordinary of themselves. That a woman lying in hypnotic sleep in a living room in Indianapolis, Indiana—a woman who had no interest in or acquaintance with musty details of obscure Civil War history—should spontaneously produce, in a coherent and fluent story, even only eight to twelve items in the life of an unknown young man which researchers were later able to verify in historical documents—is a circumstance sufficiently startling to demand some explanation.

Mrs. Williams stated that she herself would like to have more complete confirmation before she could believe that reincarnation was indeed the explanation; but at the same time she admitted being struck by two subjective evidences: 1) the fact that she could feel the expression of her face alter to the face of a youth as she lived the Donaldson experience; and 2) the fact that, as she herself put it, "during the trance I could see myself loading a cannon just as plain as if I'd been doing it right there and I've never done anything like that in my life."*

It was the intention of the Association for Research and Enlightenment (the organization formed to study the Cayce records) to make a systematic investigation of the psychological as well as the historical aspects of the case. Mrs. Williams agreed to submit to a series of formal psychological tests, some conventional and some new, prepared by a noted East-Coast psychiatrist who is interested in the reincarnation hypothesis. However, following the death of her mother, Mrs. Williams became very ill; and the project was postponed, perhaps indefinitely, because her husband began to object to further experimentation.

So in a sense the case remains inconclusive; as in the case of Bridey Murphy, there are those who will find it convincing, despite its incompleteness, and there are those who will demand a more rigorous probing, particularly into the personality dynamics and unconscious factors in the life of Mrs. Williams.

How, then, are we to regard this appearance, in so many places, of what purports to be past lives? Is this some sort of psychic epidemic, comparable to the great plagues of earlier centuries? Some kind of curious mental malady, attendant on the noxious emanations of the Atomic Age? The sly prompting of devils (as one theological school believes) whose purpose it is to bewilder and confuse the faithful? Or is it rather an epoch-making step forward toward answering the all-important question: What is man, and what is his purpose here on earth?

Consistency without collusion is evidence in a court of law. It is also evidence in the realm of science. If a great many serious and professionally trained people are independently finding the same sort of thing, surely there must be, beneath all the smoke, some fire.

Most certainly all of this strange material, from so many different sources, must be rigorously evaluated. It must be sifted of elements of fantasy, identification, telepathy, obsession, or dramatization of buried

---

*The Courier Journal, Louisville, Ky., April 2, 1958.

childhood memories. It must be weighed in psychological and philo-sophical balances. *But it cannot be ignored.*

We owe it to ourselves, to future generations, and above all to our own intellectual integrity not to ignore it.

# 4

# Many Mansions Revisited

*The life and work of Edgar Cayce have already been dealt with at some length in There Is a River and Many Mansions.* But inasmuch as some of the present readers may not have read either of these two books, a recapitulation of their contents, and especially of *Many Mansions* (since its focus of attention was more specifically on reincarnation) seems advisable at this point. The present chapter should be skipped, then, by persons who are already familiar with the latter book.

There are two principal things to be considered in the Cayce phenomenon: (1) The evidence which it provides for reincarnation; and (2) the principles of reincarnationist psychology which emerge from the data.

With regard to the evidence, the point must be established first that Cayce's clairvoyance had been directed for years only towards the healing of disease. He helped a Catholic priest in Canada, for example, to be cured of epilepsy; his own son to be saved from blindness; a Detroit business executive, who lay dying in a coma of uremic poisoning, to be up and about in a few days; a wealthy socialite to be healed of a rash around her eyes, which had baffled New York specialists; a San Francisco baby suffering from indigestion and sleeplessness to be rid of the pinworms, which were the unknown cause of his condition; and so forth and so on.

A simple list of these cures (all carefully documented and on file for the inspection of anyone who wishes to examine their validity) would literally fill pages. But a mere list could not possibly give a complete picture of the range of the Cayce clairvoyance. A study of the variety and scope of his gift, and the extraordinary validation of it, is a research project in itself which would require another book for adequate presentation. It ranges from the trivial to the important, from the insignificance of a passing remark to the drama of saving a human life.

A trivial instance, for example, is seen in the following. (It must be remembered that Cayce was lying asleep on a couch at Virginia Beach, with nothing to go on but the name and address of the person for whom he was giving the diagnosis.) He began a reading for a fifty-seven-year-old man in Oregon by saying: "Nabisco. Yes. Unless they do something rather soon for this body, we will find the heart block or the arterial block will cause a stroke, for there are clots."

On reading the transcript afterwards, both Cayce and the stenographer were mystified by the curious word "Nabisco," which seemed so meaningless and out of place. Afterwards, a letter from the man's wife, acknowledging the accuracy and helpfulness of the reading, indicated that they, too, had been struck by the word—Nabisco had been his nickname as a child.

A skeptical businessman from Philadelphia sat down and wrote a letter to Cayce in 1934, challenging Cayce to tell him who he was. He signed a fictitious name to his letter—SALOHC INOSORDEP—and gave his address in care of a local foreign consular office in the Schaff Building. Cayce, weary at this point of being "tested," and dedicated, moreover, only to the help of the suffering, refused to do as the man requested but offered to give a reading if the man actually needed physical help, and would send his proper name and address. The businessman complied with these suggestions and an appointment was made. Cayce began the reading: "Yes, we have the body here. 11:47. He has just laid aside the paper he was reading." He then proceeded to give an analysis of his own clairvoyance and explain why it was not always accurate. After having thus satisfied in part the man's purely intellectual curiosity, he proceeded to a description of the man's physical condition; described his feeling of heaviness after eating and his inability to digest food properly; indicated the cause of this condition and how to remedy it; advised that he should not eat luxurious foods ("it's expensive to the body—not the purse"); interrupted himself twice, during all this, to correct the punctuation of the stenographer who was sitting across the room taking down the reading in shorthand; and finally concluded by saying that—at 12:27—the man had just been disturbed.

The businessman had to acknowledge that from beginning to end, everything concerning him was accurate—including the fact that at 11:47 he had laid aside his paper and at 12:27 someone had come in, disturbing him.

When one reminds oneself—as one frequently needs to remind oneself in examining the Cayce work—that this entire description was of a total stranger given at a distance of, in this case, some two hundred odd miles, one realizes what an astounding thing has happened.

It is this accumulation of extraordinary confirmations that leads one to approach the past-life phase of Cayce's work with respectful attention.

Without repeating here the gradual development of this phase and the manner in which Cayce's own deep-seated skepticism about it was overcome, we shall proceed with the seven principal facts which contribute to the conviction that the life-reading material is reliable. These are as follows:

1. Character analyses and descriptions of life circumstances were correct, on total strangers, at distances of hundreds of miles and in thousands of instances.

2. Predictions of vocational abilities and other traits proved accurate in later years both for new-born children and for adults.

3. Psychological traits were plausibly accounted for by presumable past-life experiences.

4. The material was self-consistent over a period of twenty-two years: that is, it agreed with itself, both in basic principles and in minute details, in hundreds of separate readings taken at different times.

5. Obscure historical details given in the readings were later verified by consulting recorded history; the names of obscure former personalities were found in the locality where the readings said they could be found.

6. The readings had a helpful, transforming influence on the lives of the persons who received and followed them.

7. The philosophical and psychological system which is implicit in and deducible from the readings is coherent, consistent, sufficient to all known facts about mental life, and conducive to the discovery of new explanations for unexplained aspects of mental life. It also agrees with the ancient philosophical doctrine that has been taught in India for centuries.

These evidences of the validity of the Cayce material on reincarnation is by no means submitted as being "proof" of reincarnation; it is merely very strong inferential evidence. Absolute proof for reincarnation is, actually, very difficult to establish and it may require the combined evidences of photography, electronics, hypnotism, clairvoyance, and psychiatry finally to give us incontrovertible proof. It is the opinion of the present writer that within the next fifty years, if not sooner, this proof will be forthcoming.

In any case, if we take the Cayce material on past lives seriously, we can come to some rather definite ideas about the laws of life through which reincarnation operates.

The basic law would seem to be encompassed in the Hindu word karma—which means, literally, "action," and which has come to mean action and reaction, or cause and effect, in the moral world. Its equivalent in Christian terms is found in the well-known propositions: As ye sow, so shall ye reap; as ye do unto others, so shall it be done unto you.

Each new incarnation, it seems, is governed by the law of karma in such a way that the physical body and the circumstances of each successive life reflect the merits and demerits of past–life behavior.

This concept of karma is familiar to all students of Eastern thought. It does not always appear immediately in age–regression experiments. There was no evidence of it, for example, in Ruth Simmons' recall of what may have been her former personality as Bridey Murphy;* but in the extensive work in past–life recalls now being done by various professional people, karmic significances sometimes do appear.

In the Cayce readings, however, with their wealth of medical and therapeutic detail, both the concept of reincarnation and that of karma lose their general character and become more specific and psychologically real.

The following propositions can be regarded as fundamental to the understanding of human destiny and to a system of reincarnationist psychology:

1. Karma must not be regarded as purely negative. It has two aspects: continuitive and retributive.

2. According to the continuitive aspect, any action that does not go counter to cosmic economy or cosmic law tends to continue in its effects. Effort is never wasted.

3. Thus: Talents and abilities, cultivated in one life, tend to persist in succeeding lives. Sometimes their expression may be inhibited, however, by other karmic life circumstances.

4. Also: Traits of character, interests and attitudes (towards religion, race, politics, sex, animals, etc.) tend to persist in succeeding lives. Introversion and extroversion tend to persist also, unless karma steps in or unless efforts are made for ambiversion.

5. According to the retributive aspect of karma, any action that is "evil," or harmful to the well–being of any other unit of life, is exactly "punished" in a manner proportionate to and appropriate to the original harm done.

6. Three kinds of retributive karma could be distinguished in the Cayce readings:

---

*In the famous Bridey Murphy case. See *The Search for Bridey Murphy*, by Morey Bernstein. Doubleday & Co., 1956.

*a) Boomerang:* A man who blinded others in the past finds himself blind in the present.

*b) Organismic:* A man who eats to excess in one life-time can suffer from digestive weakness in the next.

*c) Symbolic:* A person who "turned deaf ears" to others' plea for help in a past life is literally deaf in the present. Or: A person who caused "witches" to be dipped in cold water in Puritan witchcraft trials suffers from enuresis (bed-wetting) today.

7. Retributive karma operates at both the physical and the psychological level.

8. Mockery and criticism of others can invoke psychological and physical retribution; one suffers the same thing that one has mocked or criticized in others.

9. Infidelity to a mate in the past can result in one's experiencing infidelity from one's mate in the present.

10. Great loneliness or isolation can result from suicide in the past.

11. Karma is sometimes "in suspension," so to speak, for several life-times. Cruelty committed in Atlantis, for example, may remain unpaid in five or six intervening lives, and may finally be met in the present life.

12. The suspension of karma seems to be necessary for three basic reasons:

*a)* The culture epoch must be appropriate to the payment of the debt.

*b)* The entity needs to develop sufficient inner resources and strengths to handle the karma.

*c)* The entity may be able to pay the debt only in association with other entities and therefore must wait until such time as they are incarnated also.

13. Mental abnormalities can be traced in some cases to past-life experiences. Thus phobias of animals, closed places, water, etc., are sometimes due to terrifying experiences or even death associated with these phobia objects.

Recurrent dreams and hallucinations can also in some cases refer to past-life experiences. Mental disease is sometimes due to possession or obsession by discarnate entities (entities, that is, who are not currently in earth incarnations).

14. Every soul has freedom of will. Freedom of will is interfered with by the karmic laws of life only when the will has been misused, selfishly or in excessive sensuality.

15. A soul is magnetically drawn, so to speak, to parents who can give it the bodily heredity and the environment it needs for the fulfill-ment of its new life task. Physical heredity exists, but it is subservient to psychic heredity.

16. The unconscious includes the record or the buried memory of every experience the entity has ever been through, in all of its many existences.

It is important to note that all these generalizations or "laws" are seen by Cayce in a cosmic frame of reference, one which acknowledges that God exists and that every soul is a part of God; that human life is purposeful and continuous, and that it operates under law; that love fulfills the law; that the will of man creates his destiny; that his mind has formative power; and that the answer to all his problems is deep within himself.

Christ is seen by Cayce to be the way-shower, the Older Brother, the Friend, the Divine Man who, after many lifetimes of his own, achieved perfection and God-realization. To achieve the Christ consciousness (which is love) is to dissolve all karma. "For love is the fulfilling of the law."

# The Body

# 5

# A New Approach to the Human Body

*If we can accept the idea of reincarnation, and the karmic psychology that accompa-*
nies it in the Cayce readings, we will see that there must follow, as the
night the day, certain important conclusions. It is inevitable that the
reincarnation idea will lead us to many changed points of view in our
interpretation of life.

One of the major changes would be in our conception of the relation
of mind to body. Although modern thinking tends to see body–mind as
a hyphenated unit, as two interacting parts of the same whole, nonetheless the materialistic concept still prevails that the body is primary;
that the mind cannot exist without the body; and that when the body
dies, the mind dies too. In the reincarnationist's view, all these concepts
need to be reversed: the body is *not* primary, either in time or in causation; the mind has existed before this body came into being; and it will
continue to exist after this body dies.

Moreover, if we speak only of body and mind, as it has been fashionable to do ever since the word "soul" was outlawed from scientific respectability, we are speaking with inadequate terms. We will need another word, whether it be "soul," "spirit," "atman" (as the Hindus call it), "entity" (as Cayce called it), or "Thetan" (as the Scientologists call it) to designate the persisting part of us that seems to *use* both body and mind.

The very word, "reincarnation," indicates by its origin the basic philosophic position that becomes necessary for its acceptance. It comes from the Latin *re* (again); *in* (in); and *carne* (the flesh); and it is related, interestingly enough, to the flower carnation, which our Caucasian forefathers so named because it was flesh-colored. The word-makers might just have reasonably coined the word "reincorporation" (back in the body, *corpore*) as back in the flesh; and if they had, the word might have been more interesting to the modern American mind.

In any case, reincarnation means that there is an immortal essence or soul which comes back to earth many times for the sake of experience, much as a student returns many hundreds of times to the same school building. For this purpose the eternal identity takes on a body of a density suitable for this realm of experience, and the body is then the protective covering or the garment of the soul. Hamlet ended his letter to Ophelia, "Thine evermore, most dear lady, Whilst this machine is to him, HAMLET"; and "machine" is as valid an analogy, in its way, as garment. It is suggestive of the Theosophical term for the body as the "vehicle" of the soul.

This concept is familiar to any person who has ever seen a Theosophical pamphlet on reincarnation, sat in on a Rosicrucian lecture on the subject, read the wisdom of the East or the philosophy of the Neo-Platonists, or stumbled on to certain poems of Walt Whitman.

But a close study of the Cayce material, and, in fact, of all clinical researches in past-life age-regressions, leads us to see that the human body, which we have so long taken for granted, is an area that requires drastic reconsideration.

There have been many ways, in humanity's long history, of regarding the body. For the Greeks it was a thing of beauty; for the Romans, a thing of power and pleasure; for the Medieval Christians and the Puritans, a thing of shame and temptation, to be denied and despised, even beaten and abused.

According to the reincarnationist point of view, the body takes on a sudden and startling new significance. It may still be a thing of beauty and power; even, in wise moderation, a thing of pleasure; but it is no longer a thing of shame and evil. For to hate and abuse a body because it contains the possibilities of evil is no more intelligent than to hate and abuse an automobile because it contains the potentials of accident.

We begin to sense the awesome significance of human bodies when we come across some particularly conspicuous example of human deformity in the Cayce files, and learn that it is the mute but eloquent evidence of some past-life crime against life.

Some of the most dramatic instances of this are found among that group of cases that we have chosen to classify as Boomerang Karma, adapting the term from the Australian weapon that can be thrown in such a way as to return to the point of origin.

In *Many Mansions* we saw the case of a blind violinist who was told that he had once, as a member of an ancient Persian tribe, blinded his enemies with red-hot irons. Another blind man was told that, as an American Indian, he had tortured white captives in the eyes. Cruelty to others in the area of the eyes, then, led to the karmic consequence of experiencing in one's own eyes the results of such cruelty—namely, blindness.

An interesting variant appears in the case of a woman who developed iritis and later in life became totally blind in one eye. In a Persian incarnation she had, Cayce said, used her eyes hypnotically, to subject other people to her will and to her way of thinking. This was not cruelty, certainly, in the same way that physical torture is cruel; but it was selfishness and tyranny, and as such invoked karmic consequence in the area which was the physical instrumentality of her misuse of others: the eyes.

A woman of fifty-three who had had a serious back deformity since childhood, and who had lost part of one finger and had her hand mangled at the age of four, was told that she was an associate of that notorious emperor of Rome who persecuted early Christians. A young man of twenty-four became paralyzed from the neck down as a result of an automobile accident; he lived in this condition until the age of forty-two, entirely dependent upon charitable Christians for every detail of his care. He too had been a cruel persecutor of Christians.

In some cases, people are born with their physical affliction, and in some cases the affliction comes to them later in life. But in either case, it is clear that the kind of affliction that the body bears is *meaningful*, not haphazard.

Cayce indicated, it is true, that in some few cases a bodily affliction was not karmic in the strict sense of the term. A man who had lost one leg in an accident, for example, was told that this was not a karmic experience but one that afforded him an opportunity for fuller spiritual growth. Perhaps this is comparable to the case of the blind man about whom the disciples asked Christ: "Who sinned, this man or his parents, that he was born blind?" And Christ answered: "Neither, but that the works of God might be made manifest within him."

So it seems that sometimes—but this very rarely—a body's defects are not retributively significant of some episode in the soul's past. However, they still remain meaningful in this sense: that the defect enables some weakness of the soul to become redeemed, or some new virtue to get its start. A piano coach sometimes makes his pupil play on a keyboard that has been covered by a long, taut scarf; but he does this, not to punish the pupil for past musical misdeeds, but rather to handicap him in such a way as to develop in him a more forceful touch and a greater confidence in estimating the position of the keys without looking at them. Other handicaps and devices can be used; but the particular handicap chosen by the coach would indicate to the discerning observer the area in which the student needed development. Similarly in the realm of the body: any gross defect of any body, whether karmic or not (and the non-karmic instances are very much in the minority), any deviation from harmony or proportion or health, is indicative of some psychic necessity somewhere.

Bodily stature is a matter that seems to be particularly meaningful, if the Cayce readings are to be believed. The cases having to do with stature do not fit clearly into any of the three classifications—Boomer-ang, Organismic, and Symbolic—into which almost all other cases in the Cayce files seem to fall, although they seem to partake of the nature of all three.

Abnormal shortness or height of the body is a physical feature which has long been recognized by psychologists as having great psychologi-cal import. Alfred Adler was perhaps led to his classical conception of the inferiority feeling (popularly known as the inferiority complex) be-cause of his own relatively short stature, and his unhappy feelings re-garding it in early life. In any case, Adler's conception of personality dynamics has this basis: all infants feel inferior to the adults around them, and strive to compensate for the feeling; but when the individual has in addition some organic inferiority, he strives even more desper-ately to compensate.

Adler did not, of course, raise the important question of why it is that some individuals should be organically inferior in the first place; but this was not his province. Besides, had he been so indiscreet as to ask the question, it would undoubtedly have been pointed out to him, with disdainful aspersions on his soundness of mind, that genes and chro-mosomes are the obvious and total cause for all human differences. "Heredity," in short, would have been at that time, as it is even now, the stock answer to any philosophic question of the whys and wherefores of human endowment at birth.

It is precisely at this point, however, that the Cinemascope of the Cayce clairvoyance projects broader horizons upon the psychological screen.

There are at least two cases in the Cayce files in which smallness of stature, both involving feelings of inferiority on the part of the person so afflicted, was the direct result of a previous attitude of haughtiness, superiority, or condescension. Through a curious reversal and objectifi-cation, the attitude of having once "looked down on" other people, and the behavior of having *used* one's own superior physique to take advan-tage of others, now made both individuals subject to being *literally* looked down on by other people.

In one case of excessive height, the person had also been condescending and haughty; this time the attitude of "looking down on" people was objectified, but not reversed, so that the individual now *literally* looked down on people—but at the same time knew himself to be at a serious disadvantage. The second case is of great interest in other connections, and will be discussed more fully later.

All of the foregoing cases illustrate how cruelty or abuse, either physical or psychological, can result in a later lifetime in a sick, deformed, or inferior body—the sickness, deformity, or inferiority being appropriate to the cruelty or abuse perpetrated; or how the misuse of one's own body, either physical or psychological, can result in a later body which is in some way inadequate or inferior. They are all illustrations of the equilibrating action of karma, in its retributive aspect.

It must be remembered, however, that karma is a neuter word literally meaning *action*, and that it has two aspects—retributive and continuitive. This is true on both the psychological level, where we see how interests, traits, talents, attitudes, etc., tend to persist from life to life, and on the physical level, where we see in many cases the persistence of various physical aspects from one life to another.

A person with a susceptibility to tuberculosis was told, for example, that this was a carry-over from a life in early America when he had contracted the disease. A young girl who had a catarrhal condition was given a similar explanation: Cayce referred to it as, "what might be termed a hang-over in the soul, the mind, and the body." A woman who all of her life had a susceptibility to injury in her left breast was told that in a lifetime long ago she had died of a sword thrust which entered through the left breast. A man born with a birthmark on his hand that looked very much like a scar was told that his hand had been cut off at that point in a previous life. Several persons who were told that they had been Chinese in a previous lifetime had features that were markedly Chinese in character, though they had no oriental ancestry in the present lifetime.

This question of appearance is a very interesting one, especially in view of the treatment given it by various writers of reincarnation novels. In Rider Haggard's *She*, for example, and in Marie Corelli's *Ziska*, we find that a person's present incarnation is described as having an almost exact facial and bodily resemblance to some past incarnation. In view of the great complexity of karma, we might at first be inclined to dismiss this as romantic fancy. However, deeper reflection and the inspection of various fragments of evidence elsewhere lead us to conclude that there may, after all, be some actual substance to the idea.

The case of Champollion is tremendously interesting in this connection. Jean Francois Champollion, the man who deciphered the famous Rosetta Stone and thus gave the modern world a key to the unlocking of ancient Egyptian history, was born in France in 1790 and early developed into a child prodigy. By the time he was sixteen he knew half a dozen oriental languages, including Syrian, Arabic, Chaldean, and Coptic. He had a passion for things Egyptian and—this is the curious thing—his appearance was markedly Egyptian. C.W. Ceram writes of him in *Gods, Graves, and Scholars: The Story of Archaeology,** as follows: "Examination of the young Francois revealed that the corneas of his eyes were yellow, a peculiarity commonly found only among peoples of the East and certainly a curiosity of the first order among western Europeans. Moreover, he had strikingly sallow, almost brown pigmentation, and the whole cut of his face was decidedly Oriental. Twenty years later he was known everywhere as 'the Egyptian.' "

We may perhaps presume that both the passionate interest in Egypt, and the extraordinary Egyptian appearance, were both carry-overs, one on the psychological and one on the physical level, of an Egyptian incarnation.

There is not enough data in the Cayce files to make many generalizations on this matter; the most we can say is this: that sometimes there is a carry-over in appearance from the most recent life, and sometimes from a further—removed incarnation, from which there also comes a resurgence of interests or of karma.

Instances such as these are obviously not karmic in the retributive sense, and they cannot be interpreted as a corrective action or a guilt awareness on the part of an Overself. They are indicative instead of *the persistence in consciousness of certain experiences,* so strong as to be translated

---

*Translated from the German by E.B. Garside. (New York: Alfred A Knopf, Inc., 1951)

once again into the physical vestment either as a trace or a scar or a racially distinguishing feature, or as a susceptibility indicative of the psychic injury or weakness still present at deep layers of consciousness.

The question may well arise, after a consideration of the many deformities, defects, scars, and susceptibilities of human bodies, as to the reason for beauty and bodily perfection.

We can, of course, infer that in beauty there must be the *absence* of the cruelty or misuse which in other cases became the cause of deformity. At least, if such karmic causes were generated at one time or another, they are not coming to fruition in the present incarnation.

But the direct testimony of the Cayce readings shows us that there are also certain positive karmic forces leading to beauty, as we can see in the following cases of outstandingly beautiful women.

One very beautiful woman was told by Cayce that in a previous life in England she had cared for unwanted children. "The pouring out of self in care for the bodies, minds, and souls of the young," Cayce said, "brought to the entity all the beauties of body, mind, and soul that it now possesses." Another beautiful woman learned that she could attribute her present beauty to an incarnation in which she had dedicated herself to music and dancing. Still another was told that in two past lifetimes she had devoted much attention to her body and its beautification—first in ancient Egypt and again in the French court.

These cases of physical beauty yield the inference that the three major sources of bodily beauty in both men and women may be: (1) absence of any presently operative karma of cruelty or misuse; (2) love, as expressed in spiritual dedications, in service, or in art; and (3) attention to the body external as such: the loving care of the body or any part of it.

All of the cases that we find, however—whether they be of beauty or deformity; whether they be retributive, persistive, or rewarding in nature—have one thing in common. In all of them, the attitudes and actions of the soul in the past have led directly to the characteristics of the body to which it was magnetically drawn in the present. In all these cases, *the particulars of bodily structure were not haphazard, but were instead tremendously significant.*

It does not seem reasonable to think that part of the body is psychically meaningful and part of it is psychically meaningless or neutral—any more than it seems reasonable to think that the designer of a sports car would make some parts of it functional and other parts meaningless or useless. A car has purpose and function, as a whole, and every minute part of it contributes to that purpose and function. Similarly with the human body. It cannot be fragmentarily significant, or significant with only a few individuals. It must be *holistically* meaningful—meaningful as a whole, and with all people.

If this reasoning is correct, we must come to the unmistakable conclusion then that the body is far more than a mere vaguely appropriate "vehicle" of consciousness. It *is* a vehicle, to be sure—an instrument of locomotion in a very real sense. But it is not a separate thing, distinct from and essentially unrelated to its indwelling person in the way that a taxicab, say, is distinct from and unrelated to the passenger that takes it for hire on a journey through town.

It is rather a vehicle that is itself the direct product and creation of the soul which is using it—almost as the cocoon is the direct product and creation of the worm which spun it. At the same time the body is also an infinitely subtle, intimate, and accurate *mirror.* It mirrors both the present and the past; in its movements and ever-changing expressions are reflected contemporary attitudes, ethics, conduct, and thought of the soul; in its basic *structure* are reflected these same psychic features of the soul's long-ago past.

Structurally, it is a condensation, so to speak, of the past; it is a container and a repository *of* habit patterns begun long ago. In fact, the Cayce material leads us inferentially to the formation of two tentative laws:

1. *Each person is responsible for the body* he *now* has *and is the direct cause of it.*
2. *The body* is an *objectification or a partial objectification of the unconscious.*

And these tentative laws lead us to many important and far-reaching conclusions.

# 6

# The Human Body:
# Key and Clue to the Human Soul

*If we accept as a tentative "law" the idea that each person is responsible for the body* he now has and is the direct cause of it, and that the body is an objectification or a partial objectification of the unconscious, we are led inevitably to a corollary: *Each human body is an important key and clue to certain aspects of the nature of the indwelling psyche.*

Both self-analysis and the analysis of other people can become tremendously more penetrating by the use of this key of thinking.

A conspicuous birth deformity—blindness, a club foot, a twisted limb, the lack of arms, or the lack of one ear—naturally gives rise to the inference, in the thinking of a reincarnationist, at least, that there was some past-life cause, probably cruelty, that gave rise to it. But the relation of body to psyche seems to inhere much more minutely and inconspicuously than this, so that any disproportionate—or proportionate—limb, organ, or feature would seem to be indicative of some correspondingly disproportionate or proportionate use of it in the past, and hence some disproportionate or proportionate attitude deep in the psyche.

Each body would seem to be stamped not with a partial, but with a total imprint of a spiritual and psychological meaning. Is it too tall? Too short? Too fat? Too lean? All this is indicative of something. Prematurely bald? A beautiful head of hair? Only four fingers on one hand? An undersized kidney? Again, indicative of something. Cases in the Cayce records give us clues: we know, for example, that both misuse and neglect of any part of the body results in its distortion or imperfection; also that loving attention and care of any part of the body results in its perfection. But in addition to physical causes such as these, there are also spiritual causes, and it seems likely that we would ultimately be led to the formulation of some kind of system of body–mind correspondences.

Students of academic psychology will at once recall that attempts have already been made on a scientific basis to show that the body, or the "constitution," as it is called in constitutional psychology, has a direct bearing upon character and temperament. Men like Kretschmer, Sheldon, Viola, and Naccarati have done years of painstaking research in attempting to show that an intimate relationship exists between the structure of the body and the structure of the personality.

Sheldon, for example, soon after publication of his first book in which he classified people into three basic body types (endomorphs, mesomorphs, and ectomorphs), proceeded in a second volume to show a correspondence between body types and temperamental types; and in a third volume he dealt with the usefulness of the body–type idea in the study of delinquency.

The work of these men is much more widely respected and used in Europe than in the United States. In this country, the attitude of most psychotherapists is the rather curious compound of acceptance plus indifference. That is to say, it seems to be generally agreed that the researches of Sheldon and Kretschmer are sound; yet in actual clinical work, their conclusions are almost totally ignored. Psychoanalytical theories are so deeply entrenched that only mental and emotional causes, generated in the first years of life, are regarded as being of caus–

ative importance or diagnostic value.

In the light of the Cayce material, however, one cannot help concluding that to ignore physique as a significant indicator and even as a contributive causal factor in mental life, and, in fact, in the total life situation, is to lose sight of something of basic and cardinal importance. Lacking clairvoyant perception, and not taking into account the intricate laws of karma that govern human embodiment, men such as Sheldon can arrive at only approximate and incomplete generalizations (a limitation shared, indeed, by those of us who, lacking clairvoyant perceptions ourselves, study the Cayce data); but they must be opening up an exceedingly fertile field for research in the future. It should be said in passing, however, that future researchers may find that thinking in terms of body–mind *correspondences*, rather than in terms of bodily *typologies*, will probably be an infinitely more fruitful approach. *Parallelism* between the various levels of being will probably be the key to discovery, rather than *groupings* on one level alone.

We are living in the age of science, and it is only scientists who can prove a relationship, or correspondence, between mind and body. But in all ages, philosophers, poets, and writers have sensed that such an intimate relationship must exist.

Schopenhauer wrote: "My body is the objectification of my will." Also: "The will is my real self; the body is the expression of the will." Spinoza taught that the mind and the body are the same thing, differing only in aspects. Walt Whitman remarked: "Was someone asking to see the soul? See your own shape and countenance!"

Oscar Wilde, in his masterful fable *The Portrait of Dorian Grey*, shows graphically how the soul of Dorian Grey becomes progressively more corrupt when his face and body—magically—no longer reveal the traces of his sins. The sins are manifested, instead, on a life–size portrait which he keeps carefully concealed in an attic room. The portrait becomes more and more hideous, while Dorian Grey remains ever young and handsome.

Among other things, the story points up not only the causal relationship between spiritual evil and physical ugliness, but also the manner in which physical disease and ugliness normally act as deterrents to the soul from committing more and more evil. The fact that Dorian does not age is also an interesting thing; the question of eternal youth is highly relevant to the whole matter under discussion here. The deformities and uglinesses of old age are undoubtedly the reflections of wrong diet, wrong conduct, and wrong thought habits; and while decay is commonly thought of as an inevitable factor of mortal existence, perhaps this is a mistaken assumption. Certainly, a soul which was in full command of itself and its powers would also be in full command of its bodily projection, and "old age" would be an impossibility.

But the matter of age and its signs in the flesh is not the main point at issue here. The main point is the meaningfulness of the body as a clue to the mind and soul of the indwelling entity.

And if we accept this premise, we realize that the philosophers and poets have very little to tell us beyond their intuitions in the matter; and the psychologists of today have almost nothing at all. The Cayce data, as usual, is profoundly suggestive, and points the way to new avenues of thought, but it is also maddeningly incomplete.

Another avenue of thought that insistently presents itself is this one: If the body as a whole is significant, it seems highly unlikely that the meaning of the body should stop short at the neckline, and that the face should be a mere chance assortment of features . . . It seems likely instead that the face must be as highly meaningful a clue to the indwelling psyche as is the body as a whole.

Physiognomy, to be sure, is and has been for some time a much despised branch of inquiry. A review of psychological research done in recent years as indicated by *Psychological Abstracts* shows that there has been practically no experimental work done in the area of physiognomy; and it is not surprising, inasmuch as college textbooks almost universally dismiss the subject with contempt. "We persist in evaluating people according to physical appearances," say the writers of one standard text, "as if phrenology and related arts of character reading had not been thoroughly discredited."

Almost every text that gives mention to the subject refers to the testimony against physiognomy provided by tests made with photographs. Twenty unlabeled photographs of men and women, for example, are given to a group of judges—in some experiments, to specialists in human relations who are accustomed to dealing with people daily. They are asked to study the pictured faces and estimate the general intelligence, or the personality characteristics (such as humor, refinement, conceit, etc.) of the persons whose photographs they are. Results are disappointing. The combined estimates of the judges tend to be more accurate than individual judgments; and certain traits can be apparently judged with greater accuracy than others; but on the whole, the estimates do not show a high correlation with the actual intelligence and character of the pictured individuals. Psychologists conclude (apparently on the basis only of these rating tests, because there seem to be no others) that there is little or no relationship between physiognomy and character.

It would seem a more cautious conclusion, however, and one in more accordance with the facts of the experiment, that these tests have only proved that people are for the most part unable to *perceive* the exact relationship between physiognomy and character. Moreover, the use of photographs is obviously a flimsy and inadequate basis for either of these two conclusions. Inner character would seem to be imprinted on the *whole* body, in three dimensions. Clues to a person's psyche are obtainable from the profile as well as the front, from the whole body as well as the face. In practical experience, all of us have made estimates of other people, on the basis of their face or body build, and frequently our estimates prove in the light of subsequent experience to have been highly accurate.

The only valid basis for a scientific conclusion with regard to physiognomy would be the sort of thing done by Sheldon and Kretschmer, who have made accurate measurement of bodily structures and then made a correlation study between the physical measurements and mental measurements obtained from mental tests.

There is a story told of a woman who, on a trip to China, found an odd medallion on a busy street in Shanghai which she liked so well she began to wear it almost constantly about her neck. Its bizarre and striking design always gave rise to interested conversation; and the woman became so fond of it she adopted it as her good-luck charm.

At a diplomatic dinner in Washington she met the Chinese ambassador who, she noticed, was observing the medallion with a faint smile upon his lips. "Have you seen one of these before, Ambassador?" the lady inquired. He admitted that he had, and then promptly changed the subject.

"Would you be so kind as to translate the inscription on it?" the lady asked. The ambassador said that he would rather not. The lady insisted. "Very well, madam," he said at last with great reluctance. "It says, 'Licensed Prostitute, City of Shanghai.'"

This little anecdote yields, as do most anecdotes, many instructive insights. For our present discussion it is illuminating in this respect: it illustrates the fact that unless we know the system of symbolism involved, a script can be directly in front of our eyes and we will remain in total ignorance of its meaning.

Ignorance of Chinese may excuse us from understanding what a medallion says; it does not justify the obstinate insistence that the medallion has no meaning.

It is conceivable that the human body and especially the human face are, like the lady's medallion, a kind of inscription: a large complicated monogram, so to speak—or perhaps a sentence—easily understandable by a master who knows the language, but almost entirely undecipherable to those of us who do not. "Till physiognomy be taught by the angels instead of men," Lavater observed, poetically, apropos this very point, "it must have infinite difficulties to encounter."*

Lavater's *Essays on Physiognomy*, incidentally, though written in 1775, can reward the reader with some extraordinary insights into the matter. Lavater, a German poet, minister, and mystic, spent a lifetime observing and analyzing the human face. In spite of the fact that he was handicapped by lack of methods available to us today, and despite the fact that he never formulated his observations into a real system, his observations are still fresh, astute, and stimulating. He was keenly aware,

---

*Physiognomy: the art of determining the character of another by the resemblances and differences between his face and our own, which is the standard of excellence."—Ambrose Bierce

also, of his own limitations. "My utmost ambition," he said, "is to prepare materials for the next age—to leave memoirs relative to my great
object to some man possessed of ten times more leisure and of talents
and philosophic genius far superior to mine, and bequeath to him, if I
may so express myself, this truth: a system of physiognomy as a possibility."

The Cayce life–reading data suggests this truth as a possibility also.
But we soon realize that there is an immense need for research: research in comparative physical and mental measurements; research in
racial features as related to racial characteristics; research in comparative medicine, psychology, physiognomy, anatomy, electronics, and anthropology. "As above, so below" is an ancient occult maxim. We lack
complete knowledge of what may be "above," in the intricate and subtle
realms, that is, of the soul and its history; we also lack complete knowledge of what is "below," in the body, in its glandular and molecular and
electrical aspects. So we are handicapped on both sides of our study of
correspondences. It will probably be many years before a true science
of body–mind correspondences can be established, and it will probably
not be done without the help of trained clairvoyants.

One clue that Cayce gives us, which is important, is that the body is
only a partial, and not a complete objectification of the soul. "In each
body," he says explicitly, in a reading for a man suffering with multiple
sclerosis, "there is projected *something of the soul self.*" He also explicitly
stated elsewhere that at conception, the parents create an opportunity
for a soul to incarnate and the pattern of genes then attracts a soul
whose needs correspond to the potentials provided by that pattern. He
added that a soul *can take on different bodies, personalities, or personality patterns, anyone of which could fit the soul's individuality, depending on what phase of
development the soul wishes to work on.*

This concept parallels the teaching of Patanjali (a Hindu authority of
considerable stature) that the body is a "karma–container"; that the mind
has "innumerable latencies" (or habit patterns, good and bad); and that
in any given incarnation only certain "latencies" which are suitable for
ripening and have the opportunity of manifesting, will combine with
each other.

If this is true, then any given body is only a *partial objectification* of the soul entity, and—like any geometrical projection—it is considerably less in dimensions than the actual thing being projected.

This may at first glance seem unreasonable; but it is, on closer inspection, very credible psychologically. A man's personality is subtly different in his office from what it is in his home; it is different as a father from what it is as a husband or as a sportsman. Each of us will show slightly, or even widely, different facets of our nature to our grandmother and to our lover. Yet the total individuality remains the same; different combinations of parts are called into play in different situations. Similarly, on a larger scale and in a more fixed manner, any given body with its accompanying personality is only a partial representation of the soul's total self.

Even without the benefits of exact scientific knowledge in the matter, we can be tremendously helped by the mere awareness that a body-soul correspondence exists. Intuitive inferences can be drawn. Both the professional therapist, studying his patient, and the average person, studying himself, can come at least to rough conclusions concerning the status of his soul from that condensation of soul which is his body.

Suppose, for example, a psychologist is presented with a child whose body is small for his age, whose hair is abnormally thin and lacking in lustre, whose lips are thin, fine, set, ascetic, not given to easy laughter, whose eyes seem withdrawn, abstracted, introverted, and whose whole appearance suggests anemic contraction. The child has been brought to the psychologist for help because of his poor performance in school, and his complete lack of friends.

On one level, the child's physique and temperament can be traced to the biological deficiencies of the mother during gestation; or to the neglect by the mother after birth; or to the economic stress on the father; or to the inadequate mineral content of the child's food.

But on another level, knowing that the soul of the child was magnetically drawn to this body by reasons of inner suitability, the psychologist can infer a spiritual causation. Perhaps, for example, the individual was a monk in a previous life. He regarded his body as unimportant, neglected to feed it properly; never washed, combed or cared for his hair—in fact, shaved his head repeatedly in the conviction that hair is an excrescence sinfully related to sexual activity. The present body is but the logical outgrowth of such attitudes and such conduct.

The inferences drawn would depend, of course, on the impressions gathered from the body and temperament as a whole, plus the measurements made with mental tests. They could be mistaken inferences, of course, because of the limitations or biases of the observer. But the more experienced with the ways of the human psyche the therapist becomes, the more likely are his rough inferences to become more refined, and more closely to approximate the truth. . Once he had decided upon some workable hypothesis, he would then proceed to work with the child with a larger horizon of cosmic intent than would otherwise be possible. On the physical level, the child would need to be given nutritional help. The hair would be given attention. The diet, exercise, posture, and general living habits of the boy would be improved. Psychologically, he would be given the usual psychological treatment indicated in such cases: better home relations, remedial reading, perhaps, special tutoring in school work; various techniques of getting along better with others.

But on the spiritual level, the therapist knows that ultimately this child must be made to see: (1) that the body is not to be despised but respected, reverenced, and made a perfect instrument; and (2) that the life of withdrawal as a monk has unfit him for social intercourse and that he needs to relearn healthy human relations on a spiritual basis.

There may be elements of spiritual or intellectual pride; or there may be elements of timidity or selfishness. There are a thousand possibilities. But in any case the physique and the physiognomy of the child has given the psychologist definite and important clues as to the needs, imbalances, and misapprehensions deep in the psyche, now called up for redemption in the matrix of the present body and the present-life situation.

The body then becomes, as it were, a Book of Revelation. In it is condensed much of our secret history. In it are latent the necessities of our future.

# 7

# Beauty as a Goal of Human Life

*Beauty is not ordinarily regarded as the proper goal of a philosopher; nor is it usu-*ally considered to be of any practical concern to psychologists, doctors, ministers, or priests to help their patients or parishioners to become beautiful. As a quest and a purpose, beauty is commonly regarded as the trivial preoccupation of beauty salons and of women whose vanity outweighs the more real and more sober preoccupations of life.

And yet—if we carry still further to its logical conclusions the data of the Cayce files—we must arrive at the conviction that beauty is of far greater significance and importance, psychologically and spiritually, than we had thought; and that, indeed, philosophers, doctors; psychologists, ministers, and priests alike should be as much guided by beauty as an ultimate goal of all people as they are by concepts of adjustment, efficiency, health, happiness, morality, and of the Good Life.

If we accept the Cayce clairvoyance, we cannot help but conclude that Keats' famous line: "Beauty is truth, truth beauty" can be better expressed, at the psychosomatic level, as: "Beauty is goodness, goodness beauty." For we see again and again in the Cayce records that ugliness and deformity are the penalty of evil behavior, and that beauty, health, and symmetry are the reward of good.

The semanticist may, to be sure, raise several important issues at this point. He may well point out, first of all, that beauty is a relative matter; and it is certainly true that different standards of beauty are to be found in different portions of the world. Extreme examples of the variability of human concepts of beauty are to be seen in the dish-like lower lips of Ubangi women—a deformity which they deliberately create—and again in the tightly bound feet of the women of ancient China. But these are extreme and eccentric examples. Generally speaking, the differences between concepts of beauty are not so great as the similarities. In almost all cultures, health, energy, proportion, symmetry, and clarity of outline are the basic components of beauty, whatever minor variations there be on the theme—and even over race and culture lines outstanding beauty is recognizable by all people. In any case, the karmic balances would be fairly made as long as the individual in question was beautiful or ugly *relative to the standards of the group in which he found himself*—so that minor differences in the criteria of beauty would probably reflect the difference between racial archetypes and not appreciably modify the karmic equation.

The semanticist may point out next that "good" and "evil" are also relative matters; and here again, his point is well taken. Morals and customs differ startlingly in different eras and different portions of the world. But, by the Cayce and the reincarnationist view at least, goodness and evil in the last analysis transcend the relativity of custom and exist in a more cosmic, more universal sense than that usually attributed to them by moral systems. Goodness, by this view, is that which is loving, unitive, kind, and spiritually instigated; evil is that which is selfish, separative, cruel, and sensually instigated.

In the Cayce files we have the case of a contemporary woman the right side of whose face was paralyzed. Why? Because, Cayce said, she had misused her beauty in an unspeakably shameful manner when she was once a queen in Cambodia. Certainly the morals of ancient Cambodia must have differed in many respects from those of today; and beauty in that era might well have meant eyes of a slightly different slant and coloring of a slightly different hue than that in favor in modern Anglo–Saxon countries. But grossness and sensuality, and the selfishness that is almost inevitably associated with them, are universals, found in all eras and all countries; and a paralyzed face is a paralyzed face: a deterrent to beauty no matter what the era or what the current fashions in beauty.

And so the general equivalence of beauty and spiritual virtue, over the arc of time, would seem to be a true equivalence, in spite of the relativity of cultures.

There is still another objection that can be raised to this equation. All of us have seen cases of inner goodness combined with outer beauty; we have seen cases where the outer ugliness was a clear reflection of the inner evil. But we have also seen cases where inner goodness was found combined with outer ugliness, and the converse where an unscrupulous or shallow character was clothed with great outer personal beauty. Moreover, we have seen ambiguous and misleading cases in the middle ground somewhere between these two poles.

There are several factors that can account for these apparent discrepancies. First, there is the subjective element: the limitations of the judge. He who is lacking in a trait cannot easily recognize its manifestations in another. He who is of lesser intelligence cannot possibly perceive the subtle gradations of the intelligence that is above him; he who is of lesser spiritual goodness cannot perceive the delicate nuances of spiritual goodness and sensitivity beyond his own. Moreover, he who is lacking in wide and deep experience of men makes generalizations on an inadequate basis. A person who has had one unhappy experience with a red–haired woman, and several happy experiences with strong-jawed men, may thereafter have a strong negative judgment against all red–haired women and a strong favorable predisposition to all strong-jawed men. Racial and national biases may make him blind to the structural beauty in the faces of persons of other racial or national origins. These limitations and biases are involved in any human estimate of another human being.

And so what sometimes seems to an observer to be a contradiction between inner and outer may not necessarily be a true contradiction; it may merely be lack of fine enough perceptions on his part to see the correspondence. We can be misled by a smooth symmetrical appearance much in the same way that we can be misled by a smoothly written contract. It is only later, when the lawyer points out to us the phrases in fine print, that we clearly see the true heartlessness of the document. Similarly, sad and perhaps expensive personal experience may lead us finally to see the minute lineaments and proportions which clearly spell treachery or selfishness in the face of what we had for a long time considered to be a completely beautiful person. And, on the other hand, it may require the combined influences of art and of life experience to make some people aware at long last of beauty in faces (especially those of other races) which at first seemed nondescript or ugly.

A second element in this whole problem of apparent discrepancy is the element of parallel causation—by which we mean that a beautiful body can be the result (according to the Cayce material, at least) of two levels of causation: the spiritual and the physical. The person who directs all his thought and energy to the creation of physical health, symmetry, and beauty will be rewarded sooner or later by a healthy, symmetrical, beautiful body; but it can well be an "empty" body in the sense that a beautiful store-window mannequin is empty. An individual of this type would seem soulless—as do, in fact, many extremely beautiful men and women. Spiritual content and intent is lacking; and persons of this type can probably find their most educative experiences in life through the loss of their health, beauty, or symmetry.

Third, there is the element of change—a gradual change of the psyche either in the upward or the downward direction from what it was at the point of incarnation.

Let us consider first the upward change. Let us imagine the case of a person who, for karmic reasons of correction, was born into a deformed or otherwise ugly body, and who in early life or midway through life, learns the lesson of kindness, tolerance, or love that he was supposed to have learned by the deformity. He becomes kind, loving, outgoing; his rather unprepossessing face becomes irradiated from within by the goodness of his spirit.

We see the radiation and overlook the structural defects—until we become analytical about it and conclude, unwarrantedly, that there *is* no parallelism between body and soul! The truer conclusion might be that parallelism exists; but what we see in looking at the face and body is the spatial, structural imprint of the unconscious mind, so to speak, *the body being parallel to the individual's former self.* The conscious mind is gradually transcending the evil of the unconscious into beauty, which beauty we catch glimpses of in the smiles, attitudes, glances, acts, or other temporal aspects of the person, but which will be completely objectified structurally only in a future embodiment. In the next life-time, perhaps, we shall see the same entity in a body that perfectly reflects the newly wrought beauty of the soul.

Because of what we are pleased to call the inertia of matter (though it may in reality be only our ignorance of how to master matter) it always takes time, in our dimension at least, for an idea to be completely ob-jectified in matter. This phenomenon is well known in the field of soci-ology, where it is referred to as a "culture lag." There would seem to be a kind of culture lag with respect to consciousness and its full objectifi-cation in body, too. Though every thought and emotion leaves its traces on the nervous system and thence, ultimately, to the surface appear-ances of the body, this is a gradual and cumulative thing; a total trans-formation cannot be seen until the time of the next embodiment.

But there is also possible a downward change—a deterioration rather than an improvement. If the person is born into an unattractive or even downright ugly body, and his reaction to his bodily appearance and other life circumstances is one of resentment and hate, bitterness, and selfishness, aggression and harmfulness to others, then the ugliness of the body will be more than matched; it will be intensified by the in-creasing ugliness of soul. In cases of this type no discrepancy is appar-ent to the observer.

But it is the contrary cases in which we see the discrepancy which is so common, and so misleading. This is the case when the soul finds itself as a "reward," so to speak, for one thing or another, in a beautiful and symmetrical face and body. The self-consciousness of the ugly or the mediocre never afflicts him. He finds himself looked at, admired, sought after. Every mirror reassures him of his own excellence; without effort on his part, almost every person he meets pays him the tribute of flattering attention.

This can indeed be a difficult test; not all souls can withstand it. Just as some people can more easily withstand adversity than prosperity, so can some more easily withstand ugliness than beauty. Many a soul can be considerate, temperate, kindly, and decent when held within the humbling restraints of an ill-favored face; that same soul, suddenly enclothed by a beautiful face, can become corrupted by his own beauty and the power that it gives him. Vanity, pride, arrogance, sensuality, self-indulgence, selfishness both active and passive, and a host of re-lated evils can easily follow. Unless an individual born to this situation has maturity of spirit or natural humility, it is all too easy for him to begin feeling a separative sense of pride with regard to beauty, and to begin to exploit it. The latent weaknesses of character and spirit can then begin to express themselves. They may be visible at first only in some altered expression of the face, perhaps, or even some more deep-lying psychosomatic consequence; but they will be completely objecti-fied in structural inharmony only in a later embodiment.

To be sure, all practicing psychologists of any real insight recognize the importance of external appearance in the formation of their pa-tients' own self-estimate. The case files of many psychologists will show remarkable psychological transformations in people who—either through plastic surgery or dental surgery or other external improve-ments to the body—have gained a self-confidence that they never had before. The case files of plastic surgeons reveal dramatic instances of the same thing. There have been instances where juvenile delinquents and even mature criminals have been led, basically, to their antisocial be-havior because of some conspicuously ugly facial feature which brought them taunts and ridicule; it is a matter of record that an altered outlook on life and improved moral behavior accompanied their altered physi-ognomy.

But the deep-lying significance of beauty, mediocrity, or downright

ugliness, the profound effect that the awareness of one's bodily appearance has on inner mental life, have never been systematically recognized by any of the great psychologists.

Adler spoke at some length of "organ inferiority," to be sure, by which
he undoubtedly understood by implication external factors of appearance also; but he did not, to the writer's knowledge at least, explicitly
dwell on the matter of appearance at any length, nor accord it the subtle
and widespread importance it actually exerts in the inner world. Perhaps it must be the task of a woman psychologist fully to explore this
area, because women are more sensitive to the importance of appearance by virtue of their being still so dependent—as objects of the male's
sexual choice—on their own attractiveness.

One example of the far-reaching consequences of the awareness of
ugliness is seen in the following pathetic letter, addressed to Mr. Cayce
in a plea for help by a forty-year-old man.

"I was born an ugly duckling," he begins, "a fact emphasized by family and associates as long as I can remember. It was the foundation of
certain unshakable inhibitions . . . Lacking the opportunity because of
appearance and temperament for normal relations with girls, I turned
within myself and definite homosexual tendencies developed. Certain
contacts then and now have inclined to emphasize these tendencies.
Needless to say, I am in a perpetually unhappy state." He goes on to
relate his failure as a teacher and in various other occupations, his con-
tracting of a serious skin condition, his repeated thoughts of suicide.

Homosexuality, perpetual unhappiness, and the desire for suicide
are serious matters indeed—and there is good reason to believe that
this case is not an isolated example of the causal relationship between
such conditions and the person's outer appearance. Indeed, it may well
be that much of homosexuality stems not only from hormone imbalance or unhealthy early conditioning, but also from the inescapable
fact of having a too-feminine or too-masculine *appearance* to be able to
assume naturally the proper role as man or woman.

Inasmuch as the man in this case requested a physical and not a life
reading, we find no comment on Cayce's part as to the past-life spiritual
origins of the ugly-duckling state which gave rise to the subject's un-

happy mental condition. Cayce recommended suggestive therapeutics, among other things, but had little to say about externals.

However, there is ample evidence to show that he did not regard externals with indifference or puritanical disapproval. When people wanted to know how to improve their appearance, he always gave them explicit answers; he gave considerable counsel on improving the skin, the hair, the figure, or the appearance in general and recommended various exercises or cosmetic preparations for this purpose.

Moreover, this advice would seem to have been given in the perspective of an ancient philosophic and occult background. Cayce had lived, presumably, in an important previous incarnation as a high priest in Egypt, in an era when two temples, The Temple of Sacrifice and The Temple Beautiful, were dedicated to both the physical and the spiritual perfection of human beings.

In the Temple of Sacrifice operations were performed, using high-frequency electrical instruments (brought over from Atlantis) to make more beautiful and perfect the human body, correcting structural deformities wherever possible. In the Temple Beautiful individuals were given spiritual and vocational guidance by trained seers, and all the resources of music, dancing, and art in general were brought to bear on the release of the highest inner potentials. Its very name suggests its orientation: beauty as both an end, and a means of achieving that end.

Possibly in the age that is dawning, an age in which light and sun and natural beauty are entering more and more into the architecture of our buildings—perhaps in this new age, light and beauty and freedom will also enter into the bodily dwelling places which house our immortal selves. Perhaps doctors will be clinically concerned as much with helping people to be beautiful as with helping them to be healthy, and perhaps they will recognize, diagnostically, together with psychologists, that any deviation from beauty, in the total body or in any of its parts, is a fact not only of physical but also of spiritual significance. Perhaps ministers and priests will begin to teach that good conduct is in reality beautiful conduct, conducive to bodily as well as spiritual beauty; perhaps classes in philosophy will spend less time in recounting the history of speculations and more time in formulating an integrated life–goal of wisdom made possible by the expanded vision of the universe given us by modern science and parapsychology, and in showing that wisdom of mind and beauty of body are, ultimately, inseparable obverses of the same reality.

Perhaps someday we shall have centers like the Temple Beautiful and the Temple of Sacrifice which will be integrated places of human healing and perfection. The total man would be the object of interest here, not mere fragments of him from the specialized and compartmentalized points of view of dentist, endocrinologist, chiropodist, or psychologist. In centers such as this all resources, both inner and outer, would be brought to bear on the creation of beautiful human beings. There would be, as in Egypt, two approaches—from within outward, and from without inward. For though mind and spirit are causatively primary, none the less a reciprocal action does seem to take place; and to work with stubborn materials—whether they be paint, stone, cloth, or the body itself—is of itself educative and disciplinary to the spirit.

In the hands of an enterprising materialist, to be sure, such a center might become a ghastly combination of beauty shop, massage and steam bath emporium, and metaphysical renovation parlor, a kind of combined super–market and Hollywood star–conditioning project. Undoubtedly, both the supermarket and Hollywood provide us with instructive examples of efficiency and all–inclusiveness; but a center such as we envision would need to be undertaken in the spirit of reverence and spiritual dedication, as it was in ancient Egypt, and not in the spirit of material profit or sensual glorification. Perhaps many decades more will need to pass before such a spirit is truly manifest in the world.

But even if such a modern temple never does appear, individual practitioners concerned with the helping of mankind can be greatly aided by an awareness of the lesson of beauty to be learned from the Cayce readings. And all of us, men and women alike, can be prompted by the long–range view of many lifetimes, to the awareness of our own obligation to strive consciously for beauty, on all levels of being.

This must be done almost impersonally, however, and without sensual attachment; in the spirit, as Cayce puts it, of "making a perfect sacrifice, holy, acceptable unto God." It must be done with the same sort of terrible compulsion that an artist feels to transfer some beautiful image to canvas, or a sculptor to capture some lovely proportions in stone. For unless it is done out of such an impersonal passion for beauty itself, and out of a kind of sense of obligation to render to the universe a gift at least as beautiful as the most insignificant of nature's handiwork, the beautiful body we create will become itself a terrible snare, trap, and delusion.

"Be ye therefore perfect, even as your Father which is in Heaven is perfect!" Christ enjoined us. And we have no reason to believe otherwise than that we must also perfect the body through which we have expression, even though we know the body to be a transitory thing.

In fact, as will appear in a later chapter, the whole intent of the enigmatic Book of Revelation is, according to Cayce, our own self-regeneration, our own redemption of our entire selfhood, including the body, so that, like Christ we achieve radiant perfection of our total being.

Edward Carpenter expressed a profound recognition of this same idea in his little-known masterpiece, "The Secret of Time and Satan."* He writes:

*The art of creation, like every other art, has to be learned.*
*Slowly, slowly, through many years, thou buildest up the body.*
*And the power that thou now hast (such as it is) to build up this*
    *present body, thou hast acquired in the past in other bodies;*
*So in the future shall thou use again the power that thou now*
    *acquirest.*
**But the power to build up the body includes all powers.**

The whole poem, and especially the last line here quoted, carries profound and far-reaching implications not fully understandable without the reincarnationist point of view; and it is deeply suggestive of the intimate creative relationship that exists between soul and body.

Sri Aurobindo's point of view is also comparable to Cayce's. Sri Aurobindo, a contemporary Hindu sage, made a diametric departure

---

*Edward Carpenter, *Towards Democracy* (New York: George H. Doran. Company, 1922)

from the traditional Hinduism which consists of such intense spirituality that all material considerations are forgotten or ignored. In his central book, *The Life Divine*,"* Aurobindo advocates that we reach the spirit
in our meditation and in our inner life, *but that we then return to the world
and transform it in the image of the spirit.* Thus all of life—all institutions,
dwellings, organizations, the human body itself—comes to be made
consciously by us in the image of God, and all of life becomes truly
divine.

There are, to be sure, many philosophic points of view possible with
regard to the proper relationship between the material world and the
world of the spirit, between body and mind; those who accept the point
of view of complete materialism, or on the other hand those who approve of world denial, body denial, and body rejection, will not find
Carpenter's, Aurobindo's, or Cayce's view acceptable.

But those who *do* find it acceptable will discover that by this viewpoint the hitherto irreconcilable pairs of opposites, matter and spirit,
body and soul, disappear—as they are disappearing, in fact, in the world
of the modern physicist. There is no such thing as "matter," really, the
physicist tells us, it is only energy at a certain level of density and in a
certain type of arrangement. It becomes our task, by Cayce's and
Carpenter's and Aurobindo's view at least, not to deny the existence of
what we call matter, or to ignore it, but rather to *transmute* it through the
alchemy of understanding and insight and effort and love into higher
levels of density and into patterns of beauty and excellence that will
match the beauty and excellence of all of God's handiwork.

---

*Revised edition; Calcutta: Arya, 1940

# 8

# The Endocrine Glands

*The importance of the endocrine or ductless glands in the human body has gradually* been discovered, in this century, by medical science. It is common knowledge now that human growth, metabolism, and reproduction are largely dependent on healthy glandular functions, and that glandular imbalance or deficiency can result in giant or pygmy stature, in obesity, in goiters, in abnormal hair distribution or fat distribution, and in physical abnormalities of one kind or another.

It is also widely known that human emotions are intimately involved with the secretions of the glands. When we become excited or angry or fearful, there is an increased flow of adrenalin into the blood which sometimes permits of prodigious feats of strength or abnormal bursts of energy. There is good reason to believe that depression or any other long-sustained emotion has definite glandular consequences.

The Cayce clairvoyance concurs with the findings of the medical profession in this area. Many physical readings attribute a condition of ill health to badly functioning glands. The readings were instrumental also in the development of a liquid gland—regulator called "Atomidine" ("atomic iodine"). After its development, through readings requested by a Hindu chemist, it was frequently recommended to people suffering from a variety of complaints with a common origin in gland dysfunction.

Perhaps the most important original contribution that Cayce makes to our thinking, however, is to suggest for our consideration the possibility that the endocrine gland system may be intimately related not only to physical and emotional conditions but also to four other areas of human life: mental abnormalities; psychic experiences; karma and past-life experiences; and spiritual experiences of an illuminative and transformative nature. What is perhaps more important, the data that he gives us is not only susceptible of scientific verification, but has already been put to test, even if on a very modest scale.

With regard to certain mental derangements, Cayce indicated that they were sometimes due to a malfunction of the glandular centers. In one serious case of violent nerve spasms and hallucinations, he attributed the condition to "the opening of the lyden gland"—a term which he persisted in using to refer to what in medical science is called Leydig's cells, just above the genital organs. In another case, classified as a manic-depressive psychosis, he diagnosed the condition as being due to "pressures existing in the coccyx, lowest lumbar, and sacral areas . . . which prevent the normal closing of the lyden gland." In another serious mental case he remarked: "There has been the opening of the lyden gland. Thus a disturbance through the glandular system. Possession at times is the result."

These abnormal mental conditions, especially cases of possession, obsession, and hallucination, were regarded by Cayce as negative psychic manifestations. On the other hand, he maintained that such experiences as clairvoyance, telepathy, and mediumship are related to the glandular system also, and should be regarded as positive psychic manifestations.

Both the positive and negative expressions depend on some unusual functioning of the glandular centers, usually involving the "lyden"

gland. He was perhaps more explicit with regard to the positive manifestations, indicating that three glands were intimately involved: the
pituitary, the pineal, and the "lyden." Together these three form, he said,
"what might be truly called the silver cord in the body." Along this silver
cord, parallel to the spine, there flows upward a stream of energy which,
when it reaches the head centers, forms the "crook of the staff" or the
"sacred hooded cobra." The pituitary then becomes the "cup that
overfloweth" and a psychic or a spiritual experience becomes possible.
His imagery in describing the phenomena will be recognized by students of the matter as being drawn partly from Christian and partly
from other sources.

He described his own psychic faculty in these same terms. As he was
lying unconscious on the couch, he explained, an "erg of energy" moved
from the sex glands upward; not until this electrical current reached the
pituitary center and "burst into light" did his clairvoyance begin to operate. At that moment, he could begin to give a reading.

People who wanted to develop psychic faculties were given a number of suggestions as to how to awaken these glandular centers. First,
however, there was always the caution given that one's purposes for
developing such powers must be pure—which is to say, unselfish; in
fact, in some cases it seems apparent that he would not give any suggestions at all to persons whose motives were tainted with selfish desires for personal power.

But to those who desired to develop such gifts for the service of their
fellowmen he had several major suggestions to make. The basic one
was meditation and prayer, together with genuine self-dedication and
the living of a disciplined and constructive life. Auxiliary suggestions
were concerned with breathing and diet; with the admonition that
dreams be carefully recorded every morning and analyzed, for dreams
are a gateway of communication with the superconscious self; and with—
curiously enough—the use of certain gem stones, notably the *lapis lingua*,* to be taped over the pineal gland on the forehead during meditation

---

*Lapis lingua*, as Cayce called it, is a combination of azurite and malachite, generally
known under the name of chrysocolla.

as a stimulus (through its atomic radiation) to the gland beneath.

These suggestions have been put to experimental tests by Hugh Lynn Cayce (Edgar Cayce's son) and by William Petersen.

William Petersen's experiments were done entirely with the *lapis lingua* stone, in combination with the Rhine ESP cards† and with drawing experiments. In the drawing experiment, one person made a drawing of some emotionally charged childhood incident, and another person attempted to pick up and reproduce the drawing through mental telepathy. *Lapis lingua* was taped over four of the glandular center areas of the sender of the drawing. An increase of six "hits" (or accurate reproductions) was noted when the *lapis* was used as against when it was not used. In several experiments with the standard experimental deck of cards, there was some increase seen when the *lapis* was used in one experiment, and no increase seen in another. Careful controls were used to eliminate the factor of "faith"—that is to say, a bag placed over the gland center on the forehead sometimes contained a piece of clay and sometimes *lapis* so that any possible increase in scoring could not be attributed to suggestibility or faith in the stone. In any case, the results of all of these tests are inconclusive, even though scoring gains were sometimes seen with *lapis*.

But the point is that the whole matter is entirely susceptible of further experiment and possible verification. According to Cayce, the priests of ancient times wore certain gems over certain portions of their bodies, not for ornamental reasons alone, but for the purpose of stimulating and bringing to highest potency the various gland centers which lay underneath.

In August, 1950, Hugh Lynn Cayce conducted at Virginia Beach a three-week controlled experiment, known for convenience as "Project X," the purpose of which was to examine the validity of the Cayce recommendations regarding psychic abilities. Seven young men between the ages of twenty and thirty-one participated, all of them college students or college graduates except one. The young men were requested

---

†This is a deck of twenty-five cards especially designed by Professor J. B. Rhine of Duke University for experiments in telepathy.

to observe a one-month period of preparation for the experiment, which included the following disciplines: (1) no coffee, tea, or carbonated drinks; (2) no smoking; (3) no heavy meats, only fish and fowl in moderation; (4) no alcoholic beverages; (5) no sexual intercourse or other sex stimulation; (6) regular sleeping schedule; (7) the reading of certain passages of the Bible and other literature of a religious or spiritual nature.

During the actual three-week concentrated period of the experiment, there were group discussions on spiritual and psychological matters, sessions of prayer, breathing, and meditation, daily experiments in telepathy using the Rhine ESP cards, the keeping of daily dream records and of journals of self-analysis and self-observation.

The results were highly interesting. There was a distinct upward trend in the scores on the Rhine telepathy cards; the dream records seem to indicate some increase in precognitive perception; and there were numerous evidences of endocrine stimulation. During the three-week period, the seven participants recorded in their journals eighty-one physical sensations in the endocrine areas, forty-three of them being in the solar plexus and thymus areas. Heat sensations were noted seventeen times, sensations of motion back and forth were noted eleven times, and circular motion four times.

But perhaps the most interesting outcome of the experiment was the release of various psychological blocks in four of the individuals involved. In three cases it was merely a greater freedom in discussing their inner problem, and a decrease of inhibitions generally. But in one dramatic case the young man in question experienced a very vivid and distinct sensation during his meditation period. There was first a terrific pulsation in the chest, making him feel as if he were smothering; then there was a lightening and a lifting and a flowing sensation rushing upward like a fountain, suddenly bursting into the head, bringing a sense of expansion. Then there was stillness.

Afterwards, the young man felt a complete sense of release from a hatred against his father which he had harbored ever since his mother's death some years before. He had regarded his father as responsible for her death, and though the two of them lived together, the boy rarely spoke. "A stranger left home," the father wrote Hugh Lynn Cayce after the experiment was over, "but a son came back." If nothing else, the case demonstrates that Cayce's general recommendations for meditation, discipline, etc., can lead not only to increased psychic perception but also to the resolution of deep-seated psychological blocks. But more is involved in the incident than this.

If we analyze the case carefully, we find that we probably cannot attribute the boy's changed attitude entirely to the strange physical experience that he had. There were too many factors operating: he had been for several weeks in a group-therapy situation; his own reading, his discussion of spiritual and psychological problems with the other young men, and the teaching and counseling of Hugh Lynn Cayce might all have contributed to his growing insight, making him intellectually aware, at least, that hate is unprofitable and even guilt is forgivable.

But the fact remains that, by his own testimony, his deep-seated hatred of his father had not been changed *until* the earth-shaking experience of his body in meditation. It was as if the tight clamp of a steel vise had suddenly been released; and for the first time in years a natural feeling of affection became possible.

The Cayce readings said that mind is in every cell of the physical body; and that the endocrine glands are focal points and storehouses of karma. In the case just cited the relationship between the boy and his father may have been karmic or it may not have been; that is to say, the hatred may have had its origin in the present life span rather than in the past. But in either case, the attitude and the emotion of hatred had apparently been congealed, so to speak, in certain areas of the body; meditation, prayer, discussion, discipline, etc., had helped dissolve the congealment; and finally a distinct physical sensation involving the glands had completely dissolved it, bringing the boy release from hatred. In short, there is seen here a clear interaction between the psyche and the body; and the body is again seen to be not merely an *instrument* but an actual representation and condensation of the psyche, through which release and "salvation" must come.

Inasmuch as the glands do seem, according to all medical science, to predetermine body size and even structure, it seems reasonable to associate the pattern of the present body with the karmic determinants of the past. And further refinements in our knowledge of the glands and their effect on temperament and emotional predispositions should enable us to see still more clearly and intricately how the total life style of the present is the direct consequence of causes set in motion in the past.

It may be that there is a concentration of memory "engrams," so to speak, or recordings in the gland centers; and it may also be that those persons who under hypnosis or other techniques can recall past lives can do so by virtue of some particular glandular sensitivity. This is a possibility at least, and a sign post in the direction of future research.

Certainly, release from psychological fixations and negativities, such as the one we have seen in the case of the young man in the experiment, is equivalent to a kind of salvation: but a salvation in a more rational sense than the usual fundamentalist and theological conception of the word. And "salvation" in this sense, the sense of spiritual self-redemption, is, according to Cayce, the real meaning of the mysterious Book of Revelation, and the glands of the body are actually the main subject matter of that peculiar book.

# 9

# The Book of Revelation

*People of the Christian faith are sometimes shocked at the multiple names that the* Hindu scriptures give to God; they conclude that Hindus worship a pantheon of gods, rather than one, and recoil in distaste at the thought.

Actually, however, each of the Hindu names for God carries a differ-ent shade of philosophic meaning and refers to a different aspect of God's infinite reality.

When we begin to think deeply upon the human body we find that here, too, one name, one image, one analogy cannot suffice to represent the full reality. This is not to be wondered at, perhaps. If it is true, as occultists have long maintained, that the body is a microcosm or small universe, which corresponds point by point to the big one, then it be-comes apparent that the body, like the universe, like God, must also have an infinite number of aspects. We can think of the body as a vehicle, as a chariot, or as a machine; as a mirror, as a reflection, as a crystallization; as a garden, as a city, as a kingdom; as a house, as a garment, as an envelope. Or we can think of it, as some people do, in more technological analogies, as an electronic instrument; as a tape-recording device; as an assemblage of electrical force–fields. None of these similitudes or labels is adequate to the reality, but all of them have a certain important validity and a certain usefulness in our learning how to understand and handle ourselves.

In carrying to its logical conclusion the data of the Cayce records, we have seen earlier how the body in its appearance and structure can be regarded as a book, legible with varying degrees of correctness by the self who inhabits it and by other persons; for the real seer, who knows the secret code in which it is written, it is a veritable Book of Revelation.

One arrives at the analogy almost inevitably, even after only a partial acquaintance with the Cayce life–reading data. But interestingly enough, one discovers on further study that Cayce himself uses the book analogy, though in a slightly different sense, in a surprising group of readings which have to do with the last part of the New Testament—the Apocalypse or the Book of Revelation.

Tom Paine called this a "book of enigmas"; another more caustic critic, Thomas Jefferson, referred to it as "the ravings of a maniac." Even the most devout of biblical students will agree that most of the book seems obscure.

There have been many conflicting attempts at systematic interpretation of this enigmatic document. The interpreters fall into four main types:

1. The "Praeterists": those who believe that it was a prophecy of Jewish history or the history of the Christian church in Roman times, and that it has already been fulfilled;

2. The "Futurists": those who believe that the cataclysmic events related in the book are supposed to happen just before or after the second coming of Christ;

3. The "Historical" or "Continuous" interpreters: those who believe that some of the prophecies have been fulfilled, some are now being fulfilled, and some will be fulfilled in the future;

4. The "Spiritual" interpreters: those who do not approve of the em-

phasis upon the time element in the other three groups, but who stress the moral and spiritual elements of the book, and read it as ideas rather than as events.

The Cayce interpretation falls more nearly into the fourth group, but it makes quite an extraordinary departure from orthodoxy.

It was in 1930 that there first appeared a reference to a hidden meaning locked within the seemingly confused imagery of the book. It appeared in a reading taken for a young girl who was suffering from a severe case of nervous instability. A description was given of the girl's physical condition, and then this remark was made: "For with pressure in the lumbar and sacral region there is an activity to those forces which operate through the pineal gland to the upper portions of the body which correspond to those forces spoken of in the Book of Revelation. It would be good for the doctor here to read Revelation—and understand it!—especially in reference to this body."

This mention of the Book of Revelation in connection with a girl's physical condition aroused the curiosity of the girl's family and of the people of the Cayce staff. But the pressure of daily work and the urgent demands of the sick and suffering precluded investigation into the full implications of this strange allusion. It was not until 1933, in fact, that the interest aroused by those cryptic words was pursued. A group of students in the Norfolk area began to obtain a series of readings on matters of general interest and it was decided to ask further questions on the Book of Revelation.

Out of this project came a strange series of readings. One is tempted, in fact, at first to discard them as an area perhaps where Cayce's clairvoyance went sadly off the beam or—to change the analogy—where his interior television set, so to speak, received only wavy lines and dashes instead of the usual clear-cut images.

And yet several ideas emerge from these readings which are attention—arresting, which seem psychologically plausible (if one's approach to psychology, that is, is on a non-materialistic basis), and which cannot be summarily dismissed when one considers them in relation to other psychological data, both from the Cayce work and other sources.

According to Cayce, the exiled John had a strange inner experience while in meditation one Sunday on the island of Patmos ("I was in the Spirit," he said, "on the Lord's day . . . "). It was an experience in consciousness, a vision; and it had to do, not primarily with a prophetic preview of cataclysmic world events, as is so frequently thought, but rather with what might be called an illumination experience, or a transformation of the self.

John proceeded to record his experience afterwards in a cipher or key, deliberately calculated to mislead those who might suppress the document if they knew its true meaning, and thus to protect its hidden message for those who might later find the key.

All the strange, fantastic talk of churches and candle-sticks, beasts and horses, elders and lambs are not to be taken in a literal or even a prophetic sense: *they refer rather to some portion of the human body, with respect to the spiritual development of its indwelling spirit.*

When John says, for example, in the fourth verse of the first chapter: "John to the seven churches which are in Asia: Grace be unto you, and peace . . . " he is actually addressing, not the church congregations scattered through Asia Minor (it seems that there were more than seven churches at that time in any case), but rather the seven gland centers of the human body: the pineal, pituitary, thyroid, thymus, adrenal, "lyden," and gonad glands.

When he says that he turned and saw seven golden candlesticks, and " . . . in the midst of the seven candle-sticks, one like unto the Son of man. . ." he means that he saw these seven centers, spiritually illumined, and the Christ consciousness active in the midst of them.

When he speaks a little later of the four and twenty elders, seated around the throne, he is referring to the head (called the throne because the higher gland centers, the pineal and pituitary, are there located) and the twenty-four cranial nerves which control the senses of the body. When he says that the "elders fell down" he means that the senses fall down or become subservient to spiritual powers.

When he speaks of the fours beasts, he is referring to the four animal aspects of man: the desire for self-preservation, food, sex, and self-gratification; when he speaks of the four horses, he is speaking of the four basic driving emotions (Cayce does not clearly specify which).

But most basically important of all is the concept of the seven churches, seven candlesticks, seven angels, and seven stars, as referring in one way or another to the seven primary endocrine centers and to their etheric counter-parts known as "chakras" in Hindu yoga; and the book with the seven seals is the human body, each "seal" or center of which must be spiritualized before it can be "opened" or vivified. When this opening takes place, the soul knows the truth of its being, and it begins to be free.

There is much more material in this set of readings, purporting to interpret the floods, thunder, earthquakes, clouds, sickles, voices, smoke, plagues, vials, etc., which are the complicated subject matter of the rest of the Book of Revelation. The details of this interpretation need not concern us here; they are an elaboration of and extension of the basic ideas already referred to, and can be absorbingly interesting only to those who enjoy the unraveling of a complicated cipher or to those who are profoundly interested in exploring the matter completely.

But for the general reader or student, the most intriguing general concept that emerges is this: that the Book of Revelation may be, as Cayce puts it, a "study of the *self*, and the self's relation to the universe and universal forces," and that the endocrine glands constitute an inner system which has profound psychological and spiritual significance, even beyond those significances which we have already seen in the previous chapter.

Sooner or later the person who accepts the concepts of reincarnation and karma asks the inevitable questions: How can we get free of the mess we are in? How can we finally get out of the seemingly endless treadmill of birth and death and suffering? How can we get loose of the tangled skein of karma? There are a number of practical answers to these questions, and we shall deal with some of them in a later chapter. But one answer at least, both theoretical and practical, is to be found— if Cayce is to be believed—in the Book of Revelation.

The first book of the Bible, the Book of Genesis, purports to be the story of man's creation. It is only appropriate that the Book of Revelation, which is the last book of the Bible, should concern itself with man's safe return to his Source. Both books have been misunderstood and have, indeed, been far from clear to begin with: what was intended symbolically has been interpreted literally, and the original wheat has also, in all probability, been mingled, through much translation and retranslation, with chaff. But if the Cayce interpretation is in its general lines correct, we see then that the "redemption" of man comes *through and in his body, involving a total transmutation of that body*. This happens not because of the sacrifice of a man called Christ, but because of the sacrifice each one of us must make of the personal ego within us to the cosmic or Christ consciousness; and when the Christ consciousness has taken over, it then transforms every cell and every atom of the body. This is not only redemption, but also a *resurrection*—each dead or unawakened cell arising to a new life and a transcendent light.

The personality of man is what passes through a regenerative process, but by immediate reflection and involvement, the body does also. "To him that overcometh," it is promised, "I will give to eat of the Tree of [eternal] Life."

In order to overcome we must have, for one thing, an awareness that *we are not the body*. The *I* within us cannot be joined by an equal sign to the body, because the *I*, the soul, the eternal selfhood, is greater than the body, which is only a partial objectification of it. But at the same time we must have the awareness that this body we are using *is* a partial projection of ourselves; it is our private project, our personal assignment, our laboratory, our chemical retort, our engine room, our field of corn. Whatever we do with and to our body is the measure of our spiritual power and intelligence. In order to make of it a perfect thing we must come into conscious relationship, downward, with every component part of our vehicle, and also into conscious relationship, upward, with our Source.

These awarenesses and this conscious relationship can only be achieved by overcoming the sense of materiality which causes us to equate ourselves with the body, and the irresponsibility, indifference, ignorance, inertia, or gross sensualism which permit us to regard the body as anything but the divine object and opportunity that it is.

We find that we can add, then, to our analogies for the body—and we do this, not as a literary exercise, but because each analogy gives us a tool by which we can better and more intelligently handle it. The body is not only a vehicle, a mirror, a garden, a dwelling place, a garment, a book, an electronic recording device. The body is also a testing ground, where stresses and strains are placed upon the psyche to determine its measure of strength, just as stresses and strains are placed upon automobiles in the giant factories of Detroit to determine whether or not they are excellent enough to be entrusted with human life.

"For each soul meets itself," says Cayce, "in that phase of its experience in which the errors occurred." The body, then, is the place obviously where the sins of the body must be faced and redeemed; and it also becomes ultimately and more subtly the place where the sins of the mind must be faced and redeemed also, because the body is the objectification of the mind.

But more than a testing ground, the body is also a developing ground, a kind of gymnasium, so to speak, where the psyche is given an opportunity to develop its spiritual muscles. And when the rudimentary testings and developments have taken place, then the body finally becomes a meeting ground—the meeting place where the human meets the divine, and there is a down flow of power (into the purified vials), and man finally feels himself to be *free* at last.

It was this final stage that John presumably experienced on the Island of Patmos, and wrote about in the Book of Revelation.

When Buddha said: "In this very body, six feet in length, with its sense—impressions and its thoughts and ideas, are the world, the origin of the world, and the ceasing of the world, and likewise the Way that leads to the ceasing thereof," he was expressing precisely the same idea that is given us by the Cayce interpretation of the Book of Revelation.

"Church!" exclaimed Tom Paine contemptuously, repudiating the rigid theological orthodoxies of his time, "My mind is my church!"

The mind can indeed be our church—and not only in the rational sense of intellectual inquiry that Tom Paine meant. But so too can the body. On the authority of Christ Himself we are told that our body is the temple of the living spirit. But because of much repetition some of us have lost the singular force of the statement. *My body is my church!* we can exclaim (instead of temple), or even, "*My body is my cathedral!*" and we can say this with new wonder, perhaps, and new realization of its import.

The body must be kept clean and holy; it must be regarded with the reverence that is due to all life; each detail of its wonderful architecture must be seen to be symbolic of some aspect of thought; and each of its intricate and beautiful parts must be regarded as aspects or stations on the spiral of an ever–evolving consciousness.

Sex

# 10

# Some Karmic Aspects of Sex

*To find oneself in a human body is to find oneself either male or female. This curious* circumstance not only makes life more interesting; it also makes it more complicated.

Sex is, as any student of advertising and publishing knows, a highly intriguing phenomenon, charged with explosive possibilities and accompanied by an infinite number of strange, beautiful, and terrible ramifications. With it are involved the most intense of human emotions: love, hate, jealousy, treachery, betrayal, cruelty, sacrifice, devotion. Suicide and murder frequently take place because of it. Life is brought into being as its consequence. Lives are dramatically and drastically changed through its agency. Little wonder, then, that sex has been the endless thematic source for poetry, song, drama, and literature of every kind in every age.

As with all other realms of human life, the reincarnation idea enables us to see sex on a far wider screen of vision, and at the same time makes clear and reasonable matters that otherwise would seem chaotic and senseless.

For one thing, we find that from an enlarged and cosmic point of view, the notion of sex being the "original sin" must undergo substantial reevaluation. The principle of sex, as we call it on the biological level, underlies the entire manifest universe. Vegetation and animal life would be non-existent without sex—and this is obvious. But it is equally true, even though less obvious, that mechanics would be impossible without its "male" and "female" aspects; so would electricity and so would the very structure of an atom. If sex—or more properly speaking, polarity—were truly a "sin," then the entire universe is sinful.

It is not sex that is a sin, any more than atomic power or electricity can be said to be a sin. It is the manner in which any principle or any force is *used* that determines whether it is good or evil.

Sex is, obviously, just as dynamic a force as is atomic energy, and the recognition of its power has led all peoples, all over the world, to put various regulations upon its expression. These regulations differ markedly in different societies and in different ages. Among the Samoan islanders, for example, it is customary for adolescent boys and girls to sleep together until such time as they decide to marry; among the Eskimos, the loaning of wives to passing visitors was at one time common practice. Obviously, what is "good" in one society is unthinkable and "evil" in another.

But the reincarnation of souls takes place over hundreds of thousands of years, and karmic action operates on lines of force that cut through all the varieties of social and sexual arrangements. It becomes apparent from the study of the Cayce files, and, indeed, from the study of the case records of anybody working systematically with age-regression, that the sex of the body, like any other aspect of that microcosmic miracle, is at the same time a trial and an opportunity, a punishment and a reward, a testing ground and a playing ground of the soul. Sex experiences, like all others, are *educative* experiences. Both joy and agony come to us because of sex, but both joy and agony are a necessary part of the enrichment and perfection of the soul.

Moreover, from the enlarged point of view made possible by reincarnation, it becomes clear that there is a universal ethics of sex which transcends the differing moral codes of various eras and places, and this cosmic code of ethics is rigorously enforced by unfailing laws of karma.

The universal ethics of sex would seem to be based on the simple formula which we see again and again in the Cayce readings: As you mete, so shall it be measured unto you . . . What you do to others, will ultimately be done to you . . . Or, as Revelation 13:10, puts it: "He that leadeth into captivity shall go into captivity: he that killeth with the sword must be killed with the sword. Here is the patience and the faith of the saints."

Sex cannot be considered in isolation: it is intimately involved with many other aspects of character.

One is given power. How does one use it? This is the test—the most crucial and basic of all tests. In a man, the sex power is usually in conjunction with superior physical force, and the test of power is twofold. In a woman, the sex power is usually in conjunction with the magnetism, in varying degrees, of beauty; and the test is also twofold. Where physical force is lacking in the man, and beauty in the woman, there is present still another kind of test: how does the individual react, having one power and one deprivation?

A woman who deliberately uses her sex and beauty as a means of self-aggrandizement, indifferent to the hurt she causes men and other women, is obviously generating karmic causes that she will have to face someday. A man who physically abuses a woman will one day, probably in a lifetime as a woman, attract physical abuse. If he shows callous indifference to the biological, emotional, or social consequences he causes a woman to suffer, he will receive the very same callous cruelty later, even if the outer social arrangements of the time be diametrically opposite. Wherever suffering is inflicted, wherever one person is exploited or his freedom of will is obstructed or his best welfare is made subservient to another's own selfish ends, wherever selfishness or sensuality override a spiritual concept of life—there a karmic cause has been generated and the price must one day be paid.

When one considers the great variety of human behavior with regard to sex, and especially of the ruthlessness and violence with which men in particular have accomplished their desires in all ages of human history, one is struck with the tremendous task of karmic justice. We have to go no further back than the Old Testament to find atrocious, incredible examples of the bestiality of men with regard to women. We read in II Samuel, chapter 13, that Amnon, the son of David, raped his own sister Tamar, and then coldly had her locked out of the house. In the Book of Judges, chapter 19, we read of a man who gave his concubine to an angry mob of men to do with what they pleased, so that they would not harm him; they abused her all night and left the man alone. Afterwards, the man rewarded the young woman for having saved his life in this manner by cutting her body with a knife into several pieces. In Genesis we read of Judah, the patriarch, who had sexual relations with a young woman and later demanded that she be burned alive for whoredom and pregnancy—until it was made inescapably clear by the bracelets he had given her that he was the man responsible for her pregnancy.

Men have not been the victim of this kind of brutality and heartlessness, except in unusual cases. We read of men being emasculated, for example, as punishment for crimes or as retaliation in wartime or because other men have wanted only eunuchs to guard their women. But by and large it has been women who have been the most brutally victimized because of sex. They have been used, abused, raped, drugged, beaten, sold on auction blocks, forced into prostitution, and treated as objects of concupiscence, discardable when no longer usable. When the full story of the karma of sex can be told, we will have a panorama that for clinical and dramatic impact will be unequalled in all the literature of the world.

It is little wonder that we read almost daily in the newspapers of sexual crimes of unbelievable atrocity. Their victims must have merited the experience from their own past–life brutality; their perpetrators must be egos of a still bestial level of consciousness who become the agents for fulfilling other people's destiny at the same time that they are unfolding their own.

In the Cayce files we do not find any particularly lurid examples of sexual depravity and crime, but we do find instances where karmic action in the sexual realm is clearly illustrated, either within or without the sanctions of marriage.

The case of an eighteen–year–old college girl in Norfolk, Virginia, is a case in point. A thirty–nine–year–old man with whom she had fallen in love induced the girl to go with him to a hotel room in one of the city's hotels. Afterwards, the man became indifferent to her, refused to see her again, and told her she should marry someone her own age. For four months the girl would not leave the house; she "nearly went crazy," her mother reported; she wanted to commit suicide. Hoping to help her "get him out of her system," the mother and brother decided to bring breach of promise suit against the man.

In the Cayce reading which the girl obtained, it was not stated specifically what she had done to merit her present seduction and suffering, but Cayce made it clear that it was exactly merited.

"In the present," the reading states, "you will find disappointments in individuals, just as you caused disappointments in the experience of others. For know: this is an immutable law! As you sow, so shall you reap! It is the sorrow and the disappointments you have caused in others in past experiences that you meet from others in your present experience. But, showing mercy, asking judgment, being patient, you may overcome."

"Would it be best for me to marry him, if he agrees?" the girl asked, in the question period. "Never!" Cayce replied emphatically.

"You mean I should never marry him, or he would never agree?" she pursued. "It would be best NEVER to marry him; your ideals would be destroyed!"

In *Many Mansions* a number of comparable instances were related in the chapters on marriage. We saw there how infidelity to one's mate in a past lifetime, for example, can lead to suffering from the infidelity of one's mate in the present. The incident of a husband who forced his wife to wear a chastity belt while he was off on the Crusades resulted in one case in the impotence of the husband, and in another in the frigidity and sexual fear of the wife.

The taking of vows of celibacy in one lifetime can have far–reaching consequences in succeeding lifetimes. By the continuitive rather than the retributive aspect of karma, frigidity or the incapacity to make a sexual adjustment usually results from such vows.

But it is when a vow of celibacy is broken that karmic penalties in the retributive sense become quite severe. One case concerns a Catholic priest and nun in England. They fell madly in love and broke their vows of celibacy together. The Cayce reading indicates that the priest dominated the woman and persuaded her against her own better judgment. It seems apparent also that their love was largely of a sensual nature.

In this lifetime these two came together again as man and wife, again of the Catholic faith. From the very beginning of the marriage the wife was frigid. At the end of the first year, the man became a helpless cripple, physically incapable of any sexual activity whatsoever.

Because of her strict Catholic views, the wife would not divorce the man, despite the fact that they were extremely unhappy together. He continued to try to dominate her mentally, as he had once before both physically and mentally. But she had chosen, in the planes between lifetimes, to go to a realm where she could develop her mind and become more intellectually independent and self-confident. Consequently, he was unable to dominate her mentally or any other way, and constant friction was the nature of their marriage.

A case like this is not to be regarded moralistically, but psychologically and spiritually. The "punishment" here is surely not to be thought of as the vindictiveness of a jealous theological God, bent on avenging two hapless transgressors of Church law. The point at issue, rather, is weakness of character in that two persons permitted their sensuality to interfere with an express dedication to a spiritual career. The man was aggressive enough to persuade the woman; the woman was weak enough to permit herself to be persuaded. Moreover, a broken vow is probably to be regarded in the same way as a broken contract or a broken word—the second party to the contract in this case being, if not God, then one's own Higher Self.

An extraordinarily painful life situation, dramatically appropriate to their own previous conduct, became the crucible in which these two souls were given the opportunity to fulfill their broken pledge, and to forge from their weakness, strength.

In the present lifetime they were brought into a situation where physical circumstances *forced* them into the fulfillment of their old vow of chastity, and into a life where there was no sensual expression what- soever. This was karma, unquestionably; but perhaps karma is related to profoundly felt guilt feelings, and to the awareness, at superconscious levels, of a spiritual task unfulfilled.

It is possible, of course, for a frigid wife to be relieved, at the con- scious level at least, that her husband makes no sexual demands on her. But in this case the woman was chained nonetheless to a distasteful situation: she was obligated to serve, constantly, a helpless, carping, and petulant cripple. For his part, the man lived almost his entire life in his mind and had no other alternative but to fulfill what had probably been his purpose before: namely, to study along religious and philo- sophical lines. And certainly at unconscious levels there must have been a deep sense of frustration, for both of them.

Karma in the sexual realm is not only an interpersonal matter, how- ever, involving other people in a retributive drama. It can also be a biological matter, involving only oneself.

Biologically speaking, the karma of sexual excess in one lifetime can result, according to Cayce, in epilepsy in a succeeding life. There is some reason to believe also that cases of arrested mental development in one life-time are traceable, in some cases at least, to sexual aberrations or excesses in the past.

The strength of the sexual drive differs, of course, with different people; what is normal sex expression for one person would be excess to another. In neurotic and repressed people, what seems to them nor- mal sex expression can in fact be actually subnormal for themselves, and only psychological help can bring them to self–understanding and normalcy.

But the point at which actual excesses begin is not so difficult for an individual to determine for himself. Each of us comes to sense this point with regard to food, and each of us can similarly sense it with regard to sex. Moreover, sex excesses almost inevitably involve other people, and any extreme is more likely than not—by mere force of mathematical progression—to cause physical and emotional hurt to others. A good criterion for the degree to which sex can be expressed is always: What effect will my gratification have on another person, or other people? And if the answer is: *It will hurt someone else*, one's course of action becomes clear—one refrains.

Thus the reincarnation principle can affect our thinking and conduct with regard to sex in several important ways. It can serve as a deterrent to brutality, exploitation, and selfishness in the sexual realm, because we know that karmic law brings us exactly that which we give to others. It can also serve as a deterrent to excesses of sex because we know that excesses can lead to epilepsy, mental retardation, and other crippling conditions. It can make us doubly thoughtful with regard to the taking—and breaking—of any vows, but especially those having to do with chastity. Vows can be made on mistaken assumptions, on a basis of fear, ignorance, and insecurity, rather than on a basis of truly enlightened insight, and they can easily lead to rigidity and crystallization. But what is worse, broken vows can lead to guilt feelings of the profoundest sort, and the subsequent necessity to make the vow good, sooner or later.

"The love of economy," Bernard Shaw once remarked. "is the root of all virtue," And at the earlier stages of virtue, this is unquestionably true. In the later stages, however, one is not deterred from evil only by fear of consequences, or by the realization that it is uneconomical, in the long run, to do wrong.

Finally the sense of personal economy drops out of the proposition, and we come to realize that love itself is in reality the root of all virtue. But this is spiritual love: love of the best welfare of all other living creatures, including those little creatures whose cellular forms provide us with the body we use; love of the great Creative Energy and Beauty which we call God. And sex is evil only when it goes counter to this kind of love.

# 11

# Some Psychological Aspects of Sex

*It seems that all of us have been men in some lifetime and women in others. At least,* sex change is generally accepted as a fact by most believers in reincarnation, such as Buddhists, Hindus, Theosophists, Rosicrucians, and others; and the Cayce readings, as well as the age-regression experiments of many investigators, provide confirmation for those who accept their validity.

No regular pattern of change is deducible from the Cayce data, however; it seems that one can be a man for one or more lifetimes and then a woman for one or more lifetimes, and so forth and so on; but what causes such changes, or when they occur, does not become clear by the Cayce data at least.

But the mere fact that we *do* change is itself of epoch-making significance, psychologically speaking.

For one thing, it can shed much light on the whole problem of homosexuality. Homosexuality can probably not be attributed to any single cause, but rather to one of several possible causes—and this is true at the medical and psychological level as well as at the karmic.* However, if indeed we *do* change sex from life to life, then it becomes clear that the very fact of change can be a basic explanation for many, if not most, such deviations.

Many cases in the Cayce files indicate that a recent change in sex can result in what might be called a psychological hang–over. That is to say, a person who has just become a woman, after a series of four or five lifetimes as a man, may well have such pronounced masculine tendencies as to find it difficult, if not impossible, to function as a woman is supposed to function, physically, psychologically, and socially. Homosexuality can be the result. Similarly, a person who has just come into the masculine polarity, after a lifetime or series of lifetimes as a woman, may find it extremely difficult to play the masculine role.

This idea can be therapeutically of tremendous value to homosexuals, and even to persons who, though not outright homosexuals, are uncomfortable or ill at ease in the sex in which they find themselves; it points clearly to the areas of thinking and behavior that most need development or modification.

The matter of sex change can also shed light on another psychological area: namely, the much disputed problem of the Oedipus complex.

Freud's notion was that every male child desires to possess the mother sexually and to kill the father; and similarly, every female child desires the father and hates the mother.

Cayce never commented on this whole matter directly, but there are two considerations here that are very thought–provoking.

According to Buddhist writings and particularly according to *The Tibetan Book of the Dead,*' it was anciently believed that just before being

---

*In *Many Mansions* there is reported the case of a man who, as a cartoonist in the French court, mercilessly made fun of homosexuals. This time he became one himself: the karma in this case being the boomerang type of karma due to the psychological cruelty of mockery.

*Bardo Thödol. *The Tibetan Book of the Dead,* translated by W.Y. Evans–Wentz (New York: Oxford University Press, 1927)

drawn again into incarnation, an entity sees visions of mating men and women and he is drawn magnetically to that pair which can give him the flesh and blood body he needs for his own life–pattern require-ments. But if he is to be born as a male, the feeling of maleness comes over him and simultaneously a feeling of intense aversion for the father and intense attraction for the mother. The opposite aversion and attrac-tion would take place in the case of an entity who was to be born as a female.

If there is any truth to this ancient idea, it would certainly constitute an intelligible basis for the whole Oedipus theory.

But with the aid of the Cayce data we could go one step further. Most normal people, the Freudians maintain, sooner or later "resolve" the complex—get over it, to use simple language. Thinking in reincarnationist terms, we could imagine the case of two persons, a father and daughter, for example, or a mother and son, *who were lovers in a life before*—and who loved so intensely that deep in the unconscious the carry–over was still very strong.

In cases like this, it could easily be imagined that the universal sen-timents of same–sex aversion, other–sex attraction felt by all entities just before being drawn into a body would *not* be easily resolved, if at all, and some form of psychological aberration would result.

On the other hand, we could also reason this way: if the ancient Tibetan and Buddhist doctrine is *not* true, and the aversion to the same-sexed, and attraction to the opposite-sexed parent is *not* a universal phenomenon, then the cases on which Freud based his Oedipus and Electra theories must have been cases in which the individuals involved were lovers in a previous lifetime. He then mistakenly erected a univer-sal generalization on what more properly should have yielded only a partial one. He said: "All boys love their mothers and hate their fathers" when more accurately, in reincarnationist terms, he should have said: "Some boys love their mothers and hate their fathers because they (son and mother) were lovers in a life before. "

In either case, the phenomenon of sex change and change of role becomes a highly significant factor in our thinking. It is the persistence of certain psychic attitudes, despite the change of bodies, that is the crux of the matter here.

In *Many Mansions* we saw how, by the continuitive aspect of karma, talents are carried over from one life to another; how attitudes towards race, religion, politics, and the opposite sex can persist from life to life also. These attitudinal carry-overs can be general: as, for example, hatred for religion in general, or sympathy for the underdog; or they can be very specific: as, for example, love for or hatred for some specific individual.

The carry-overs persist despite the change in sex in the individuals involved, or despite the changed role in a family situation or otherwise. Two brothers who became enemies in the past, for example, because one of them won the girl that both of them loved, were born as father and son this time, and a bitter hostility characterized their relationship from the very beginning.

Attitudinal carry-overs such as this could explain many otherwise incomprehensible antagonisms and sympathies among people, and particularly so in the marriage or the sex relationship.

There would seem to be, moreover, a certain temperamental polarity that is basic to many human relations and especially to the sex relationship, both because of biological and cultural factors that have existed for many ages. A theory of the psychologist William McDougall can be very instructive in this connection.

McDougall, in an attempt to account for the manic-depressive psychosis, argues that there are two basic innate modes of response typical of all human beings: (1) the self-assertive and (2) the self-submissive. An individual reacts submissively with regard to his parents, shall we say, assertively with regard to his wife, submissively with regard to his employer, and assertively with regard to his dog. The normal person is able to make all these adjustments of attitude with the same fluency with which he would go from one gear to another in driving his car. If, however, he tends to act submissively with regard to all persons and all situations, or if, instead, he tends to act always with extreme self-assertion, he is going dangerously in the direction of abnormality.

The manic-depressive psychosis is, according to McDougall, a form of breakdown occasioned when the individual, through either of these

exaggerated tendencies or through rigidity in making natural transi-
tions from one to the other, has lost touch with reality. His mental illness then proceeds with exaggerated bounds from the depths to the
heights of emotion, in excessive swings from self-submission to self-
assertion, thus revealing, as so many abnormalities do, the normal
mechanism on a magnified scale.

We are not at present concerned with manic-depressive psychosis, or
with the truth of falsity of this theory of its origins; but McDougall's
division of basic disposition into self-assertive and self-submissive is
extremely interesting and extremely helpful in analyzing the Cayce data
having to do with the relations between the sexes.

In modern America, of course, women have an unprecedented economic freedom and independence. There still does not exist full equality of the sexes, even in America; but such rapid strides are being made
in this direction, there are so many career women and there is so much
self-assertion among women that it seems almost absurd to say—even
remembering her biological role—that the role of woman is one of self-
submission.

But we must bear in mind that this economic liberation, and the
democratic ideal of equality between the sexes, is of very recent and
even almost regional growth. Only fifty years ago in this country it was
impossible for women to vote; and there are still millions of women all
over the world whose condition is essentially the ancient one of submission rather than assertiveness. In the light of these facts, it seems
safe to say that the basic disposition of self-assertiveness has, throughout much of human history, been equated with the male, and self-
submissiveness with the female. Sadism can be regarded as the extreme
of ruthless self-assertiveness; masochism, the extreme of self-submission.

If, then, we see by the reincarnationist view that one's sex and one's
role in life are constantly changing, we can see that the permutations
and combinations of assertiveness and submissiveness must lead to
many curious psychological situations. Such situations in the marriage
relationship, in fact, appear frequently in the Cayce readings.

There are many cases in the Cayce files where a husband and wife in the present have been in the relationship of father and daughter before. These antecedents, observable in dozens of cases, sometimes have favorable and sometimes unfavorable consequences. In general, such a situation seems to be favorable to marital harmony, because the pattern of dominance—submission which is typically that of a parent–child situation is identical with the traditional culture pattern of dominance—submission in the husband–wife relationship.

In the following case, for example, we see a favorable consequence. The woman in this case is the daughter of a famous American writer, and the widow of a distinguished European artist. She asked in her life reading whether she had been united with her husband in previous lives. She was told: "More than once. In the Danish experience, he was only a friend. In the Egyptian experience, he was your father. In Atlantis, he was your husband." The woman writes, in a letter acknowledging the receipt of her reading, "I was very much impressed by the statement that in a previous incarnation my husband had been my father, because there was a certain element of that quality in our relationship even in this life."

It should be noted here that the attitude of self–submissiveness which was deeply ingrained in the Egyptian parent–child experience persisted through the less emotionally charged experience of friendship in Denmark and came down to the present as a continued sense of the woman's looking upward as to a superior. It is also of interest to note that the woman in this case was four years *older* than her husband, so that one might almost have expected a motherly attitude on her part rather than a daughterly one.

In other cases, however, the unconscious pattern of parent–child relationship was one of antipathy rather than sympathy (because of a tyrannical element in the dominance); the results in the present husband–wife relationship were, therefore, unfortunate. One case is that of a Polish–born woman who asks: "What has been my relationship in the past with my husband? Why have I feared him?" The answer was: "In the Mohawk Valley experience there was an association as father and daughter; he then kept the entity well in tow." Another case is that of a marital relationship so difficult as to result in a nervous breakdown on the part of the wife. The husband's attitude had constantly been one of cold domineering tyranny, which took subtle rather than obvious forms. According to their readings, they were father and daughter in early Williamsburg, and the stern authority of the parent then was fiercely resented by the child. The pattern of domineering tyranny on the one hand, and resentment on the other, never relented into consideration on his part, nor forgiveness on hers; consequently, the same situation had to be met again, though in a slightly different form.

An interesting case of a previous mother–son relationship is to be seen in the case of a famous and wealthy American industrialist who was refused a divorce by his wife for many years. Unable to win his freedom, he proceeded to live with and support another woman with whom he had a deep bond of sympathy and understanding, a woman of quick intelligence and wide culture. She was his confidante in matters of business and was solicitous both of his health and his tastes in food. She was told: "In the Atlantean sojourn, he was the son of the entity. And the whole of the relationship in the present often bears just that same aspect, as the entity mothers his ideas and his welfare."

Frequently a husband and wife were previously associated in exactly the same husband–wife relationship. This exact repetition of role is apparently very common. If the dominance—submission pattern or the equality pattern has been well established by such previous marriages, the present marriage adjustment is very probably a relatively harmonious one. No conflict of attitude polarity is likely to arise unless other disturbing factors or karmic problems are present. There is no need, then, to dwell on these cases at any length here, though we might note in passing one rather curious case. The woman was told by Cayce that she had been traded in marriage in early Virginia for 2,000 pounds of tobacco. When she asked about her previous relationship with her husband, she was told, "He was the one who bought you! Doesn't he act like it at times?" The wife's comment on this was simply: "He sure does!"

In many cases, a previous male incarnation of the wife militates against successful marriage. This is very distinctly observable in the case of a woman who was united with her present husband in the same relationship several lifetimes ago. In the life just previous to the present one, however, she took incarnation as a man. From this male incarnation she carries over a very pronounced desire for domination and independence, together with a man–like strength of purpose that will brook no opposition. Their present marriage has been one of continuous strife almost from its inception. The partners have divorced and remarried twice. The excessive drinking, which has become the weakness of both, is a symptom as well as a contributing factor to their friction. Basically, one major difficulty is the pronounced self–assertive tendencies of both. If one or the other, or both, could achieve sufficient grace of spirit for a sufficiently long period of time to curb his own self–assertive attitude and be patient of the eruptions of self–assertion in the other, the marriage could perhaps be salvaged.

In other cases we see the reverse situation: namely, one in which the husband has made a recent change in sex, and consequently has a tendency to be feminine and self–submissive in outlook. In one case, for example, that of a somewhat effeminate man who is the father of three children and suffers acutely from sexual maladjustment, the Cayce reading indicated that he had had two previous lives as a woman, one in early America and one in France during the Crusades. The Crusade experience was particularly traumatic; the entity had been betrothed as a young girl to a man who soon afterwards went to the Holy Land. "Knowing little or nothing of the duty of matrimony, the entity's whole experience was filled with suppression and fear of sexual relationships. The entity was well on in years before these fears were removed."

We have, of course, only skimmed the surface of this whole area. The Cayce files contain any number of cases illustrative of one or another of the many possible permutations of sexual role, as do the files of other researchers also.

The basic fact of sex transposition is of importance, first, as an explanation for many strange undercurrents in human relations, particularly as related to love and hate, dominance and submission; and second as an indication to us of the cosmic lesson that we all need to learn.

Life seems almost to be like a school for actors: the director of the school wishes each student to be so flexible and so complete, as to be able to play *all* roles equally well, and for this purpose makes everyone,

willy-nilly, play widely different parts, no matter what his natural incli-
nations. Were you superb as Puck last night? Very well, then, tomorrow
you must begin to learn the role of Shylock. Were you magnificent as a
man last life? Very well, then, next life you must learn to be a woman.

In psychological terms, we must learn to be neither too self-assertive
nor too self-submissive with regard to other people, no matter what
our role in life. No matter what opportunity for dominance presents
itself as an enticement and justification to our ego, no matter what
situation of oppression seems to overwhelm us into slavery and insignificance, we must learn to be as unaffected by the one as by the other.

To our temporary inferiors, we must fulfill our responsibilities of
leadership or instruction or support; to our temporary superiors, we
must act with due respect, obedience, or compliance; but in the former
case we must not become unduly self-exalted, and in the latter case we
must not become unduly self-abased.

The abrasions and agonies of marriage are intended to polish us of
our crudities, bring to the surface our latent strengths, teach us to become more self-assertive if we are too self-submissive, or to become
more self-submissive if we are too self-assertive.

Positivity and negativity are complementary parts of the whole universe and of God himself. To become godlike, then, and universal, we
must become both positive and negative; we must become completely
androgynous.

In this, as in all other respects, the purpose of the universe is that we
shall become justly poised above, as the *Bhagavadgita* puts it, the Pairs of
Opposites; bestride, in Madame Blavatsky's profoundly gnostic phrase,
the Bird of Life . . .

# 12

# Sex: Some Implications

*Thinking in reincarnationist terms in the area of sex results in some important clari-*
fications, psychologically and ethically, as we have seen.

But perhaps the most important and drastic outcome of our thinking
in this way is the realization that by the fact of sexual alternations, *the*
*absoluteness of the sexual cleavage between men and women disappears.*

We are spirits, Cayce tells us, entrapped and enclothed in bodies. The
spirit is in the image and likeness of God; and the spirit must therefore
include both polarities within itself even as God does; it is bisexed or
androgynous in its essence, and it takes on a specific biological sex only
in human embodiment.

This concept has important and tremendous results both for our
understanding of men and women, and for our evaluation of each
other.

With regard to our understanding, it seems likely that we will be led to see that the polarity of the body conditions the psyche. In an obvious way, of course, the body's sex determines the biological and social role that one plays in life, and thus conditions the whole life experience; but more subtly than that, it would seem to have an effect upon abilities, personality traits, and large areas of mental and emotional life.

The way the body conditions the psyche is comparable, perhaps, to the manner in which clothing affects us. Every woman knows, certainly, the psychological effect of the clothing that she wears. A pair of heavy oxfords, a short woolen skirt, and a cardigan sweater, for example, give a woman's psyche an entirely different "feel" than high heeled silver slippers and a bouffant low-cut evening gown. Men do not experience as much as women, perhaps, these subtle psychological differences that clothes impart because, for one thing, men's clothing, in modern times at least, is not so varied, and for another, men's success in life is not so dependent upon the success of their personal appearance. But men experience enough of a psychic difference between the wearing of dirty old fishing togs and a tuxedo to know that clothes *do* affect one's morale, self-esteem, self-estimate, and consequently have ramifications in one's conduct and speech, even if only in minor ways.

How much more profoundly, then, must the sex of the body affect the psyche! And its sex, let us remember, includes more than the conspicuous or "primary" sex differences, concealed by fig leaves or draperies, and its positivity or receptivity with regard to the sex act. It includes also the "secondary" sex differences—the body's hardness or its softness, its straightness or its roundness, its distribution of hair and of muscle and of flesh. And it includes, in fact, every cell of the body, because of the direct distribution into the blood stream of differently sexed hormones, so that the body's sex is actually an all-pervasive and not merely a mechanical and localized difference. These differences cannot but condition profoundly the life-feeling of the entity inhabiting it.

Certain traits of character and capacities of mind might well be facilitated or inhibited by the sex of the body one happened to be in. For example, both on mental tests and in actual life performance, entities in the male polarity show higher capacity for mathematics and mechanics, and entities in the female polarity generally show higher capacity in language and social understanding.

These distinct differences may be acquired rather than inborn: that is to say, they may be—and probably are, in large part—the direct result of environmental influences and the pressures brought to bear because of what we think men and women *should* do. But if there is any inborn difference, then this difference *cannot* inhere in the soul as a soul, because all souls are androgynous and have been in bodily form in both sexes many times.

The difference might then arise from the polarity or the constitution of the male or female body as such. For example, dexterity of the fingers is greater in female bodies than in male because of the female's smaller fingers. Color blindness, which is much more prevalent in males than in females, is traceable to sex-linked genes. Mathematical and mechanical abilities are not so obviously related to a male body as is finger dexterity to a woman's smaller fingers, or color blindness to sex-linked genes; but perhaps, in some as yet unknown way, there is a relationship just as distinct.

The body's sex, then, would seem almost like a modality or mode of being—comparable perhaps to major and minor modes in music. In the minor mode, as in the major, certain notes and intervals *must* appear by virtue of the mode, and other notes and intervals cannot. Each has its own distinctive feeling and force and beauty; neither could, by any stretch of the imagination, be called superior to the other.

And this brings us to what is perhaps even more important than the matter of how the body conditions the psyche, namely the matter of evaluation, and the notion of superiority on the basis of sex. According to the reincarnationist view, any notions of superiority or inferiority in the basis of sex must of necessity disappear. They must disappear for two reasons: first, because they are untenable, and second, because they are so karmically dangerous.

If I have been both a man and a woman, and you have been both a woman and a man, how can either of us claim to be superior because of our sex? Superior to whom? When? The alternation of roles obviously gives us a fluid situation rather than a static one; only a moron could maintain that people sitting on the left side of the bus are the absolute superiors of those sitting on the right, when at any time in the course of his life he might be under the necessity of sitting on either one or the other side, and when all persons who ride the buses experience the same necessity. Thus any superiority attitude is seen to be, in the last analysis, absurdly untenable.

But more than untenable, both logically and psychologically, it is actually downright dangerous.

Since the time of Adler we have heard much of the inferiority feeling, and how important it is to overcome it. But the superiority feeling has not been so much discussed, despite the fact that it is equally as un-healthy as the inferiority feeling, and can lead to many terrible aberra-tions of conduct.

Wherever there is strength, wealth, beauty, power, talent, or excel-lence of any kind, the superiority feeling can easily develop, and many women have certainly been as guilty of it as men. But history shows us that in almost every civilization of which we have any record, men *as a class* have been much more guilty of it than have women.

It is easy to see why this is so. In primitive, materialistic societies, might makes right, and the strongest can easily impose his will on the others. Because of their superior size and muscular strength, and also because of their greater biological freedom, men have easily established a dominant position over women, and have perpetuated it by laws, customs, and superstitions of infinite variety and even—ironically and tragically enough—by religion.

However much the great world scriptures may have been "inspired," nonetheless they were obviously filtered through the male brains of their transcribers, and their male–dominant sentiments are very appar-ent in the texts.

Hindu, Buddhist, Mohammedan, Judaic, and Christian scriptures, to mention only a few, all show this distinct bias. "Women are as impure as falsehood itself," writes Manu, the Hindu lawgiver; "Day and night women must be kept in dependence by the males of their families."

Buddha only reluctantly, and after much persuasion, allowed women to become members of his monastic order—and then only on condition that a woman devotee, no matter how many years of service she had given to the order, would defer to a male monk, even if he had become one only yesterday.

Among the Jews, the rabbinical prejudice prevailed to the effect that woman is not capable of profound religious instruction. Better burn the Law, was their teaching, than teach it to a woman. How can man that is born of woman, asks Job, be clean? And while Christ seemed to have been free of male–domination sentiments, both the Old and the New Testament writers, especially Paul, were not. The psychologically damaging effects of their own fear and distrust and disparagement of women are incalculable in the world of men and women today.

Until very recently, women all over the world have had little better status in many places than property and animals, and in almost all places have been regarded as inferior beings. Both laws and customs have operated almost entirely in the favor of men and to the disadvantage of women; she has been denied education on the grounds of inherent mental inferiority and the right to vote for the same reason; she has in many places no right to own property, or to obtain a divorce for just cause, even though her husband could divorce her for any reason whatsoever; adultery has been overlooked entirely in the case of men, and punished with severity ranging from stoning to death to ostracism in the case of women; she still receives in many places—including the United States—less pay for the same job that men do; she is still barred, openly or through subtle subterfuges, from many positions and professions. It has only been in the last fifty years that women have been gradually freeing themselves from these injustices.

"The saddest thing in life," runs a Japanese proverb, "is to be born a woman." And if one reads thoughtfully the history of womankind, not only in Japan but in almost every country of the world, one cannot help feeling the poignancy of the saying. Women have suffered untold and untellable indignities, physically, emotionally, mentally, and spiritually because of men's compulsion to be superior; and they still continue to do so.

A situation such as this can only be accompanied by profound psychic imbalance and unhealthiness, not only in the victims of the subjection, but also in the perpetrators of it.

Philip Wylie makes this point with singular force in his brilliant novel on the relationship between the sexes, *The Disappearance.** He dramatizes the terrible dichotomy between man and woman by a science-fiction kind of story in which, presumably because of atomic disturbances, all the men suddenly disappear from the world of women, and all the women disappear from the world of men. Separate, they try to continue life as they knew it; both men and women soon realize the indispens-ability of the other sex, and learn a new kind of respect for it. But mainly it is the men who must learn how deeply they have sinned.

His principal character, Gaunt, realizes this most intensely. He writes:

> [Man] . . . became so entranced with himself that he never found enough objects of odious comparison to satisfy the greed of his inner conceit. He went to war with other men exactly like him-self, always on the grounds of their "inferiority." Not satisfied even by that, he declared another war on the still more similar half of his own tribe: woman. She was necessary to him, so he could not exterminate her, but he put her in her place to give his own a more exalted seeming. . . .
>
> If the sexes so revile each other, how can a species love? How, if one sex regards itself as superior, can it refrain from detesting the "inferior" sex? And how in the name of nature and of God can beings regarded as inferior by their mates bear towards those mates a whole affection? Creativeness is not possible where the creators are at such odds, and have been for hundreds of centu-ries. A hate of life is inevitable.

In debasing and vilifying woman, Gaunt concludes, man has de-based and vilified himself. But the added dimension of reincarnation shows us that the manifestations of a superiority complex have serious psychological consequences, not only to the present personality in the confines of the present world scene, but also indefinitely into the fu-

---

*New York: Rinehart & Company, Inc., 1951

ture. From the evidence of the Cayce files, whatever we do to another, ultimately comes back to us; as we sow, so shall we reap; as we mete, so it is measured out to us again.

The karmic law is inescapable. If the ego waxes fat, it can only mean that it must later be slenderized, through suffering; if an ego exploits its position, and treats others with contempt, with selfishness, and with tyranny, then some day it will receive the same kind of treatment itself.

Women who are suffering today, even in modern relatively enfranchised America, because of the brutality, selfishness, and subtle or obvious tyranny of some man, may find it a source of some comfort to think that they are paying the just price for their own brutality, selfishness, or tyranny of ages ago when, as a man, they treated some woman in the same callous manner.

And men of today who can see any reasonability whatsoever in the reincarnation idea should seriously take stock of their own behavior and their own subtle attitudes as well as of the legal and social behavior of all men towards all women; for if they do not, they are inviting, for some future experience of their own, as women, exactly what they are giving out today, as men.

We can have a healthy, wholesome, sane civilization on this planet only when all ego-inspired notions of superiority shall have disappeared among men and women, and the more cosmically necessary view of our complementary nature has taken its place.

# Race

# 13

# The Question of Race

*To be in a body not only means to belong to one sex or another; it also means to* belong to a "race." And, just as the reincarnation principle throws into new perspective the body as a whole and that particular aspect of it called sex, it also throws into new perspective the whole crucial and urgent question of race.

Up until the middle of the nineteenth century, it was commonly believed by people who accepted the Hebrew scriptures literally, that human history began with the creation of man in the Garden of Eden in the precise year of 4004 B.C.

There may still be some sects of Fundamentalist Bible interpreters who believe this. A belief of this kind, however, can only be maintained by refusing to acknowledge various tangible facts made available by geological and anthropological researches. Fossil human skeletons unearthed in the past century conclusively show that human beings have existed on this planet for hundreds of thousands, perhaps millions of years. The biblical stories of man's origins may be true, to be sure, on a symbolical level, but they cannot be taken in any literal sense and certainly cannot be calculated on in exact numerical terms without going contrary to evidences of the most incontrovertible kind.

According to Cayce, evolution is proceeding through many lines or streams of life on this planet: insect, fish, plant, and animal, to name but a few. Man is evolving also; but originally "man" was created or perhaps emanated as a group of spiritual beings. Hovering about the earth plane, these spirits became entranced with the animal bodies they saw and—largely perhaps from curiosity—they began to push themselves into animal forms and to mingle with other animals sexually. *This was the celebrated "fall of man": not sex as such, but the bestiality of a divine creature having sexual relations with animals*—a kind of sodomy, in short, on a mass scale. In this way the spirits became entangled with materiality, subject to animal laws and animal evolution, even though they were, as theologians might put it, a "special creation," and were not, in the true sense of the word, animals. The widely prevalent tales of half-men, half-horses, half-women, half-fish, and other such monstrosities which abound in mythologies everywhere, may then, in the light of Cayce's account, have some basis in fact; the Egyptian man–animal figures and the mysterious Sphinx itself (half-man, half-lion) may have been intended as reminders to man of both his divine and his bestial history.

At any rate, Cayce continues the account by saying that to meet this serious emergency, God created the form of "Adam" as a way of escape for the entrapped spirits; and Adam was "projected" (to use Cayce's term) on the earth at five different places at the same time. These five "projections" apparently were the archetypes for the five major distinguishable races: white, black, red, yellow, and brown, each one offering a special kind of opportunity, physically and spiritually, for development out of animality. The souls had the opportunity of expression through whichever racial type was closest to hand.

This strange account would seem to correspond roughly—very roughly, we must admit—to the two differing accounts of man's creation found in Genesis,* though the explanation as a whole bristles with difficulties and raises almost more questions than it answers. Certainly we have no way of knowing at present whether it is completely true or not. If it were true, of course, it would neatly reconcile the "special creation" with the evolutionary point of view; it would also provide a workable (if fantastic) hypothesis with which to attack many hitherto seemingly unrelated problems in mythology, anthropology, totemism, psychology, religion, and the human unconscious.

In one respect at least, however, the Cayce data parallels the findings of geologists and anthropologists: both affirm the vast antiquity of the human race. The Cayce data, however, injects another consideration, namely that this tremendous span of human history has not been on as primitive a level as has been commonly supposed.

Most histories of the world devote their first chapter to Stone Age men and prehistoric times; their second chapter plunges immediately into the great accomplishments in art, architecture, literature, and religion of ancient Egypt, dated for its beginnings at 4000 or 5000 B.C. and considered the world's first great civilization.

If the Cayce clairvoyance is to be believed, however, then Egypt is far from being the world's first civilization, humanity's first step out of savagery. It is the first civilization, to be sure, of which any historical traces have been found; but it was preceded by the rise and fall of many another civilization, equal to and even surpassing our own, which flourished long before the time of the pyramids and the Temple of Karnak.

Why do we not know of them? Because their traces have been washed away, submerged under the waters of first the Pacific and then the Atlantic Ocean. Because the great flood, to which not only the Christian Bible but most tribal legends all over the world refer, was a historical fact, not merely a myth or a spiritual symbol.

The continent of Atlantis was a fact, too, according to Cayce, and not a myth; it reached heights of technology, power, and depravity unknown even to us of the Atomic Age; yet its airplanes, its submarines, and its solar power stations disappeared under angry waters together with its

---

*Gen. 1:27 and Gen. 2:7

fantastic buildings and its high–powered people in 10,000 B.C. (just as Plato said), in the last of three successive catastrophes.

Some of its survivors escaped to Peru; some went northward from Peru to North America; some escaped to Spain; and some went into North Africa, where they intermarried with the native African Negroes. This mixture of Atlantean and Negro resulted in what we know as the Egyptian race and civilization.

The history of Atlantis, Cayce said, extended for about 100,000 years before the final cataclysm which destroyed it. He referred also to the existence of Lemuria, a continent presumably submerged beneath the waters of the Pacific; and it seems that Lemuria (the land of the "brown" race) existed some 700,000 years before Atlantis (the land of the "red" race). . . .

This is a staggering perspective; though as one reflects upon it, the idea of such a stupendously long human safari upon this planet is not an unreasonable one, either from the historical or the geological point of view. Moreover, when one considers the present point of intelligence and capacity of the highest representatives of the human race on this planet, it seems psychologically reasonable that these human souls, in their vast evolutionary pilgrimage, must have gone through hundreds of lives in hundreds of places on earth.

It soon becomes apparent, also, from any random sampling of the Cayce files, that all of us have belonged in the past to many different races and nations. We find a British woman whose past three lives were as a German, as a Jew, and as a black; a young man of Italian extraction who was formerly a Norseman, a Russian, and a Persian. A wealthy Portuguese broker of the present was a British–American, a Persian, and an Atlantean before. A noted Hindu lecturer was, in his past two lives, an Englishman and once again a Hindu. A Jewish girl in the present was German in nationality and Catholic in religion in the life just preceding this one; she became in that lifetime a Sister Superior in a Catholic orphanage.

Alternations like these are found everywhere in the Cayce files. Jews have been Gentiles, and Gentiles, Jews; Nordics have been Latins, and Latins, Nordics. Orientals have been Occidentals, and Occidentals, Orientals. Apparently no black ever had a life reading from Cayce, so we have no data on their previous lifetimes. But white Americans with Anglo-Saxon surnames have had past incarnations in Abyssinia and Africa as blacks, or in Egypt as Egyptians (who were mulattoes), as well as in every other race and nation. They have been Mongolians, Chinese, American Indians, Japanese, Hindus, Spaniards, Italians, French, Russians, or Norsemen. So it would seem reasonable to conclude—and, in fact, it is inferentially necessary—that all souls experience incarnations in a wide variety of races, colors, and countries. The generalization is supported, moreover, by age-regression experiments done by many workers in this field.

One soon begins to wonder what determines racial change or racial persistence, and whether there is any pattern of frequency in any given racial group. There is not enough material in the Cayce files to answer these questions. Sometimes there is a succession of several lifetimes in the same race: Jews are sometimes found to have been Jews several times before, Germans to have been Germans, or Danes to have been Danish, etc. But in many other cases there appears no such repetition; and we have in general no way of knowing whether Cayce merely omitted such lives because they had no particular bearing on the present life problem, or not.

Perhaps, as in the matter of sex change, there is no definite fixed pattern of race change; perhaps the needs of the soul, as correlated with the opportunities provided by different hereditary possibilities, determine where a soul should appear on earth. Race and sex would both seem to be subservient to the primary problem of developing soul *qualities*—each race, with its ideologies and cultural patterns and religious traditions providing a favorable milieu for the development of, or redemption of, different types of thought patterns in the psyche.

In any case, it becomes clear that anyone who accepts the idea of reincarnation cannot, with impunity, despise at wholesale any alien race or nation; for if he does so, he thereby runs the risk of despising his own past or future self.

It must constantly be remembered, in the matter of race as in everything else, that man *is* a soul and *has* a body, which he uses. He is *not* a body which may or may not happen to possess a soul. A proper under-standing of this relationship of soul to body is essential to the under-standing of the Ancient Wisdom, and essential to the practice of true spirituality. It is also the first intellectual step towards a tolerance that shall be thorough and scientific rather than superficial and sentimental. When one recognizes that the body is merely the transitory expression and vehicle of the soul, one must of necessity see that to despise a man for his race, nationality, or color, is as absurd and unreasonable as to despise an actor for the costume he is wearing.

The longer one reflects upon the matter, in fact, the more does one's sense of separativeness and self–importance tend to dissolve. For if my soul has incarnated in black bodies and white, in red bodies and brown bodies and yellow; if each of these peoples has at one time or another been the creator of great civilizations equal to, comparable to, or even superior to our own, in the great moving kaleidoscope of history; if I participated in those colors and those civilizations, whether as an infe-rior or a superior member, whether as peasant or prince, whether as moron or as mastermind—how then can I remain smugly convinced of the unique importance and superiority of the race or nation to which I happen to belong in the present?

*I am an encloser of all the races; I embrace, within myself, every nation, every people!* we might well exclaim . . . *I am a part of all; all are a part of me . . .*

To be sure, there are some people whose prejudices are so deeply rooted in the emotional need to feel separate and superior that no knowledge of any kind can change their convictions or their behavior in the matter of race.

There are many people who, even believing in reincarnation and intellectually accepting the idea of their own multicolored, many-nationed past, still are secretly or openly convinced of their present superiority by virtue of being, for example, a high–caste Hindu Brah-min or a white, Protestant Anglo–Saxon. To learn that they may have been anything else in their past is discarded by these people with the same kind of mental mechanism which enables a *nouveau riche* to forget his bourgeois origins and to detest his former associates. To be exactly what they are is obviously, to them, the apex of all that has gone before, the crowning achievement of all the ages.

This attitude is, in fact, quite widespread, even among occult students (some of them believe that the "Great White Brotherhood" or "Masters of Wisdom" work only through Great Britain); but it simply cannot be sustained if one honestly faces, first, various facts of science and history, and, second, certain spiritual considerations.

The facts of science include, first of all, the contribution made by modern psychology. Mental tests have conclusively demonstrated that all major planetary races have equal capacities in intelligence and talent. Blacks do *not* have inferior mental capacity; neither do members of Mediterranean countries or any other country that happens to be non-Nordic.

The facts of history supplement the psychologists' findings by showing that environmental and cultural forces play an important part in determining the rise and fall of any racial group, and its ascendancy at any given point in time. When Julius Caesar landed in Britain in 54 B.C. he found the Britons in a very primitive state of development. "Do not obtain your slaves from Britain," the Roman writer Cicero wrote to a friend, "because they are so stupid and utterly incapable of being taught that they are not fit to form a part of the household of Rome." Even as late as the ninth century a learned Arab commentator described the Anglo-Saxons as barbarians without refinement and culture. The one-time philosophic and aesthetic ascendancy of the Greeks, on the other hand, has now given way to comparative insignificance.

Cultural relativity is known to all students of anthropology; all races have "equality" in the span of time. But the majority of mankind is either ignorant of these facts, or completely impervious to them when informed. Their ego, in short, encloses them. They are living, in Philip Wylie's telling phrase, by the laws of conceit rather than by the laws of truth.

Moreover, there is an important spiritual consideration which can only be touched on here but which will be dealt with more fully in a later chapter. This has to do with the widespread fallacy, current in our times, that the I.Q., the mind, is the sole criterion of superiority. Mind can devise ingenious inventions and a great technology; but mind can also be merely the tool of cunning self-interest and the desire for power. If untempered by love, it can become neurotic, degenerate, and even fiendish. Love and spirituality are equally as important criteria of superiority as is mind.

Even granting, then, that some groups of people on our planet might be less active mentally and technologically than others, those same groups might well have a much more profound spiritual life and a much more deeply developed love nature. The Samoans do not have North American technology; neither do they have North American neuroses. The Mexicans may not come up to American standards of plumbing; neither are they guilty of American Babbitry and Coney-Islandism. The Chinese may be lacking as far as radio, television, and movies are concerned; but they also lack our shocking figures for juvenile delinquency.

Cayce indicated explicitly that *every* racial group has its virtues and its faults, and went so far as to indicate the major sin of several modern nations. The sin of England, he said, was "the idea of being just a little bit better than the other fellow." The sin of France, "the gratifying of the desires of the flesh." The sin of China, "quietude—just as in India, the cradle of knowledge not applied, except within self. What is the sin of India? Self—not selfish—just *self.*"

"Is it so strange," he remarks elsewhere, "that nations were made? No. For there must be every type—otherwise where would be the opportunities for all to manifest God in the earth? It is indeed not strange that we are given the Protestant churches: Methodist, Christian, Baptist, Congregational, etc.; for it is to meet the various needs. What is God? All things to all men, that all might know Him. There is not one better than the other."

It is with churches as with races. Each meets a psychological and spiritual need of its members. Each must be respected. Each must be seen as a matrix for the jewel that will one day become the great diamond-bodied Self.

# 14

# Race and Karma

*Egocentricity is not an easily dissolved defect of character; neither is race pride, which* is only egocentricity writ large. But the dissolvement of any form of egocentricity must ultimately take place, and life has a way of achieving this end through an infinite number of devices.

It is possible, of course, for race conceit to express itself in barely perceptible forms. Many a person who would never dream of lynching a black, for example, nonetheless secretly or openly regards himself as the black's superior. Many a person who would hesitate to put up a sign reading "No Chinamen or dogs" still regards himself as the unquestioned superior of Chinamen.

But race pride and prejudice all too frequently *do* express themselves in outer acts, ranging from small acts of rudeness or exclusion all the way to flagrant injustice and brutality.

In either case, whether silent and secret, or openly and flagrantly expressed, race conceit will ultimately be taken care of by the laws of karma.

Karma operates in such a way, it seems, that our every act and thought is exactly repaid in its own coin and in its own realm. If we do harm to another, physically or psychologically, we later suffer exactly the same kind of pain that we caused; if we haughtily feel ourselves superior to other people and treat them condescendingly, we may later find this attitude objectified by the humiliation of a body that is too tall or abnormally short—or we may find ourselves one day the member of a minority group that is despised by the majority; if we do injustices to groups of people, we are likely to suffer injustices later through the agency of comparable groups of people. Christ's command to do unto others as you would have others do unto you is not merely a sentimental exhortation, but actually the elliptical statement of a mathematical equation and a law of psychodynamics.

Let us consider, for example, the Cayce reading on an investment counselor of New York City, who was born in a town in southern France. It reads in part as follows:

"The entity was in the land. . . when the children of promise passed through the lands that they were forbidden to pass through, except with permission. The entity was among the descendants of Esau . . . The name was Jared. The entity took advantage of a group. Hence expect a group to take advantage of you! For what you measure must be measured to you again; you must pay every whit of what you measure to others. And this applies in the future as well as in the past. Do you wonder that your life is such a mess?"

It is not specifically indicated here that there was any racial element in the situation, though there might well have been. But the case is instructive and highly relevant to the present discussion nonetheless. *The entity took advantage of a group. Hence expect a group to take advantage of you! For what you measure must be measured to you again. . . .*

Another dramatic case of the same type is that of a Jewish woman of Hungarian origin, aged fifty-five, who was, at the time of her Cayce reading, working in a shop in New York City. She was very unhappy in her job; the hours were long; the pay inadequate to her need; the work distasteful to her; yet there seemed no escape from it. An interesting explanation for this relentless situation appears in the account of her preceding incarnation, in an early period of American history.

"Then the entity, in the name of Rachel Fould, was engaged in activities with groups who prepared and preserved furs, and was the companion of one in authority.

"In this experience the entity used her position not wisely or too well. Though she had material blessings, she did not show any consideration to those who labored long hours, as to their surroundings. It brought material satisfaction. But did it bring contentment or joy?

"You are reaping in the present experience this phase of what was sown. Do not think that the Lord has brought it upon you. For what you sow, you reap."

Once again there would seem to be no element of race prejudice or injustice in this situation. But once again we see an illustration of the fact that if an individual manifests grasping, callous, heartless qualities with respect to groups of people, he will someday receive exactly the same treatment in return.

The moral for all of us is clear. If we discriminate against a man because his pigmentation is darker than our own, if we refuse to give him an equal wage or equal opportunities for education, travel, beauty, and mere decent living standards, if we refuse to sit next to him on a public vehicle, if we humiliate him in a thousand subtle and obvious ways so that he comes to cringe before us in our presence and loathe us for our smug arrogance in our absence, if we exploit or humiliate others who, by the accident of history or the working out of karmic law belong to a racial group that is in a vulnerable position, the tables will be exactly turned on us someday. We likely shall someday, in some future civilization, find ourselves the member of some minority group, humiliated, rejected, ostracized, and despised. We shall likely bear the stigmata of our spiritual ugliness in some visible and unmistakable way, even as a black skin is today regarded in some places on the planet as the badge of exile.

It is entirely possible, of course, that *some* blacks of present-day America and South Africa are paying some karmic debt for their own intolerance or enslavement of others in the long–distant past. They may have been among those Atlanteans, for example, who, Cayce said, made slaves of large groups of people. This possibility is a plausible one, though it may not necessarily cover all cases.

We should remember that even though former mistreatment is likely to lead to future incarnation in troubled circumstances, the logic doesn't necessarily work in reverse. Some souls may choose out of love to in–carnate into a persecuted race in order to serve and help in the midst of trouble.

But it does seem highly inferable that many present–day blacks, and in fact members of other minority and persecuted races, are paying the price for their own intolerance, cruelty, and exploitation in past eras, whether in the black race or in some other. Yet we cannot assume that present difficulties are always a direct result of past–life misdeeds, and thus cannot pass judgment or condemnation on any individual, race or group. The Cayce readings repeatedly stress the need for forgiveness and reconciliation.

A white southerner who violently detested blacks to the point of founding a society for the supremacy of the white race, was told in his life reading that this hatred stemmed from a lifetime when, as a captive oarsman, he was so brutally treated by a black overseer on one of Hannibal's slave ships that he died of the brutality.

This is only one case, to be sure; yet it is quite conceivable that many another rabid anti–black agitator has suffered comparable experiences. But this is hardly a good excuse for such behavior and certainly does nothing toward healing the karmic memory.

In the light of these considerations, the dramatic justice and the psy–chic necessity of the contemporary scene become very clear. *Finian's Rainbow* made the point beautifully: in a clap of thunder the white skin of the bigoted, reactionary Senator Rawkins Billboard (of the State of Missitucky) was changed to black; after two weeks of living as a black, unable to enter a restaurant or even a church because of the law of the South, his viewpoint underwent some drastic changes.

Reincarnation may offer to members of persecuted groups and races of today one way of further understanding the difficulty they face. The key is to understand that we each build for ourselves, as souls, the experiences of a lifetime. A soul who now is persecuted may have been a persecutor in a previous lifetime. The current conditions serve to teach in a dramatic way, not to punish.

It is resentment and hatred directed toward those who exert supremacy that can keep this soul lesson from being learned. Surely an individual or a race which bears the burden of discrimination can work persistently and courageously for social justice. Real healing of these ancient human wrongs is possible when the victimized individuals combine a sense of soul responsibility for helping create the problem with an equally strong sense of determination to lovingly bring change. What a powerful force for change it would be if resentment against those who ignorantly exert supremacy were dissolved in the sudden realization that outer things serve inner purposes.

On the other hand, the possibility that the situation of the blacks or other minority groups is a karmic one does not justify those of us who belong to a dominant race in pursuing a flagrant course of injustice and discrimination, violating both our Constitution and our Christian principles. "For it must needs be that offenses come," says the Bible, "but woe to that man by whom offense cometh!" And again: " 'Vengeance is mine!' saith the Lord."

If we substitute the word "Law" for "Lord" we find that the sentence even more clearly indicates how man cannot justify ill treatment to others on the grounds that they "deserve" it, karmically or otherwise. Ignorant men in their ignorance may become the instruments of the Law or of the Lord; wise men seek to function rather on the level of love and of wisdom, letting life itself take care of the offenders.

There is an interesting anecdote about a man who took the ticket the ticket agent gave him, picked up his change, and walked away from the window. A few minutes later he returned and said to the clerk, "You gave me the wrong change."

The clerk snapped, irritably: "It can't be rectified now. You should have called my attention to it at the time you bought the ticket. Next, please."

"Well," replied the man, with a shrug and a faint smile. "I won't worry about it then. You gave me ten dollars too much." And he disappeared into the crowd.

The clerk's rudeness, based on a sharp awareness only of his own convenience and self-interest, rebounded to his own disadvantage, and with embarrassing immediacy. Usually the rebound is not so immediate; but it is clear by the karmic principle that spiritual rudeness on the basis of race conceit and race prejudice must have a similar result. In race injustice, as in any other injustice, we ultimately shortchange only ourselves.

But there would seem to be another kind of karmic penalty for racial animosity, of an even more intimate kind than the painful one of outer circumstance. This penalty is psychosomatic, and it results from the fact that no constrictive emotion can be long entertained without having its constrictive effect upon the body. This has been clearly demonstrated by psychosomatic specialists. Hatred, bitterness, resentment can result in a wide gamut of bodily consequences: heart disease, hardening of the arteries, diseases of circulation to name but a few.

Though bodily consequences immediately accompany every emotion, their cumulative effect does not become visible sometimes until the lapse of considerable time. Ordinarily we see the consequences in one lifetime. But if, as we have seen, the body of the present is in intimate relationship with the past; if it projects certain elements of the unconscious, it becomes clear that the body we are born with can pay the penalty in lack of health and beauty for the hates and resentments of past lives. "All illness comes from sin," Cayce remarks, uncompromisingly; and in cases as diverse as gallstones, arthritis, failing eyesight, tuberculosis, heart conditions, etc., etc., he has traced the origins to an emotional state such as resentment, hate, malice, jealousy, spite, selfishness.

"Those who hold animosities and grudges," he remarks elsewhere, "are building for themselves that which they must later meet in confusion."

It becomes clear then that a racial animosity, even if it results in no flagrant act of aggression, can ultimately damage its entertainer in a very serious way. Both the overdog and the underdog need to remember this. Smouldering resentment and hate against injustice can have just as serious consequences as the bullying fury of the unjust aggressor.

There is nothing more humanly natural than to hate another human being who has brutally raped our sister or wantonly destroyed our home and savings, all in the name of his racial superiority. Yet even this natural hatred is, in the long run, uneconomical. To hate a man because he has been stupid, cruel, wanton, and brutal is in a sense no more intelligent than for a high school student to hate a second grader because he does not understand algebra. We do not hate a stone for being a stone; we accept it as being in its appointed place in the hierarchy of nature. Similarly, it is wise, when suffering injustice at the hands of the callow, the shallow, and the brutish to remember that they, too, are stones—and on a rudimentary level of understanding on the evolutionary scale. And at the same time, those persons who like to think that the white race is in the highest bracket in a hierarchy of races would do well to remember that the callow, the shallow, and the brutish are so prevalent among that race as to cause gentler races the world over to regard them with distaste.

Still another consideration enters into the picture. Cayce clearly indicates that not only the thing we fear comes upon us, but also the thing we hate. Apparently hate is as powerful a magnetic force as love. One of two cases in point from the files concerns a man who in a past life, as a Mohammedan, hated the Catholic Church, and in this life found himself very intimately involved both by birth and by marriage with Catholicism. The other case is that of a woman who in a previous lifetime bitterly hated drinking—and this time finds herself faced with alcoholism in the family.

One cannot but think of Coleridge's poem, "The Ancient Mariner." The poem gives us a vivid picture of a man who, having unnecessarily and cruelly killed a friendly seabird, is visited by supernatural agencies with a dreadful punishment. All of his sea companions die; his ship is becalmed in the middle of the ocean; for seven days and seven nights he knows not only the horror of being surrounded by his dead companions' bodies, but also the horror of being surrounded by slimy loathsome sea creatures that swarm about the ship.

He prays for release, without any answer to the prayer. Finally, in the extreme agony of loneliness and terror, he begins to watch the sea snakes and to see for the first time their strange and glossy beauty. A "spring of love gushes" in his heart, Coleridge says, and all at once, in an unaccountable impulse, he blesses the sea snakes and their presence. In that same moment the curse laid upon him begins to lift. The blinding realization comes over him that *to pray is to love* . . .

> *. . . He prayeth well, who loveth well*
> *Both man and bird and beast.*
>
> *He prayeth best, who loveth best*
> *All things both great and small;*
> *For the dear God who loveth us,*
> *He made and loveth all.*

The experience of the Ancient Mariner is the story of every man whose heart is hard and separative and cruel, of every man who hates, with reason or without. One day, an unutterable agony of mind and body will bring him to see the beauty in the forms of life that were once repulsive to him, or a matter of indifference.

The Cayce readings give us no explicit instance of the kind of transformation that took place in "The Ancient Mariner" in the area of race dislike or race hatred; but the tenor and implication of the readings as a whole point inescapably in the same direction. Do you hate the blacks? Or the British? Or the Irish? Or the Puerto Ricans? Or the Jews? It would behoove you not to! Because if you do, you may find yourself one day either one of them, by birth, or intimately in their midst. . . dependent upon them. . .involved with them in such a way that you will come to see their virtues and their beauty, and to love them. Ultimately, you will have to achieve the capacity to love the beauty and the good in *all* peoples, in *all* races, in *all* species. . .

For in reality we are One. The mind may differentiate; but the mind is the slayer of the real. With the eyes of the spirit there is only Oneness, unspeakably beautiful, unspeakably a thing of wonder.

# Balance

# 15

# Balance: The Golden Mean: The Razor's Edge

*Certainly there is nothing new in the thought that balance is important in human* life. As long as men have been riding horses they have known that balance—equilibrium—is essential to successful horsemanship. Whether a man have for his sport swimming, bowling, wrestling, tennis, or golf, he knows that balance is necessary for good form and good performance.

Balance in the sense of proportion or symmetry was known to the ancient Greeks; in fact, principles of balance in this sense have been applied consciously or instinctively throughout all the history of art by any artist worthy of the name.

The idea of justice has been symbolized for many centuries by a seated figure holding a pair of scales or of balances; and in the same connotation we speak of being weighed in the balance and found wanting.

So if we say that one of the most significant ideas to emerge from the reincarnation data of the Cayce files is the idea of balance, it might well seem, at first sight a contribution of little originality or importance.

And yet, though the concept is not original, it appears here in a new, important, and dynamic frame of reference. In fact, the word takes on an almost transformative power if we dwell on its full implications long enough.

The idea first appears in the Cayce readings having to do with physical health, and one of its primary applications has to do with diet. Cayce's insistent counsel in this regard ran parallel to the growing realization among medical men of the importance of a balanced diet. His concept did not differ radically from those currently held by most authorities in the field: the necessity of a proportionate distribution of necessary elements such as proteins, fats, starches, and carbohydrates to satisfy all the needs of the body. He recognized the importance of an acid–alkali balance, and pointed out that persons leading sedentary lives need more alkali–reacting foods and fewer starches and sweets. He also agreed with the view, more and more widely held, that fried foods, refined sugars and starches, carbonated drinks, and artificial foods generally are to be avoided. The whole question of diet is an interesting one and the Cayce material in this area can be studied with profit; however, it is not our principal interest here, except insofar as it has to do with balance.

Balance is stressed in the physical readings in still another sense: namely the balance between assimilations and eliminations. In one physical reading he says:

"This condition has to do with the assimilations and eliminations of the body. This should be a warning to all bodies as to such conditions; for if the eliminations and the assimilations were kept more nearly normal in the human family, the days might be extended to whatever period as was so desired; for the system is *built* by the assimilation of that which it takes within, and is able to bring resuscitation as long as the eliminations do not hinder ... When eliminations are coordinating, and assimilations are coordinating, the physical body is a normal, healthy body."

Much disease could be avoided, he makes clear in a number of similar passages, if there were more complete eliminations of waste materials through all the eliminatory systems of the body, and it was to this end that he so frequently recommended colonic irrigations, sweat baths, and the like. Moreover, the life of the body could not only be indefinitely prolonged, as indicated in the above passage, but—what is equally important—could be kept young and beautiful if there were no accumulation of wastes in the cells and tissues.

These ideas are corroborated by the findings of Alexis Carrel in regard to the problem of aging. Carrel points out that if the cells could be kept clean of the accumulation of wastes—if the intake, in short, did not gradually outbalance the outgo—there would be no slowing down or aging process, and no structural changes. The chicken heart which he kept alive over a period of years was kept alive because of the optimum conditions for cell life artificially created, and the perfect balance of the two processes, ingoing and outgoing.

A third application of the idea of balance is seen in Cayce's repeated allusions, in diagnosing a variety of conditions, to "an imbalance between the sympathetic and cerebro-spinal systems." To correct this imbalance a variety of methods was recommended in different cases, including physical adjustments by osteopathic or chiropractic physicians, diet, hydrotherapy, electrotherapy, etc. The data in these cases is sometimes of a technical nature and therefore of little practical use to the layman, except suggestively, though it could be very helpful to physicians in both the diagnosis and treatment of disease.

However, the concept of balance in the first two senses—namely, a balance in diet and balance between intake and eliminations—can be a practical guide to all persons in their daily living. Every man can be his own physician in a sense, or rather his own preserver from the need of a physician, if he takes to heart this counsel and devotes some study and attention to the matter.

In a reading taken once on spiritual healing, Cayce said: "The physical body is an atomic structure subject to the laws of its environment, its heredity, and its soul development . . . If in the atomic forces there comes an overbalancing, an injury, an accident, there are certain atomic forces destroyed or others increased . . . Then it becomes necessary to bring a balance about each of the atomic centers. . . ." He goes on to say that no matter what method of healing is used, a resuscitation of the atomic centers and thus the restoration of balance must be achieved.

On the basis of this and numerous other comparable passages, one might well conclude that balance is the cornerstone of a philosophy of health and of healing.

But health is not only a physical problem; it is also psychological. And on the psychological level, too, balance is important, not only in one but in many senses of the word.

For one thing, it soon becomes clear that no psychological extreme is healthy. The Greeks knew this long ago; Aeschylus, Sophocles, and Euripides all wrote tragic dramas on this very theme. Buddha discovered it also: neither excess of pleasure nor excess of asceticism led him to the peace and enlightenment he sought. The middle path, the way of moderation, seems to be truly the way of wisdom.

Most thoughtful and relatively mature people will agree that this is a reasonable idea; but even those people who recognize its reasonability can consciously or unconsciously violate it in their own lives. It usually takes repeated painful experiences even to realize the folly of excess in so obvious a thing as overeating. Many people have suffered more than half a lifetime of painful indigestions and nauseas before they have learned, once and for all, not to eat too much fudge or too much potato salad. Many other people pay for the learning of temperance with chronic or acute disease.

How much more difficult is it then for people to learn moderation with respect to intangibles of the mind and spirit, where extremes do not always punish us so immediately! What makes the matter all the more difficult is that even those qualities that are commonly regarded as virtues can be practiced to excess also. And, partly because we have been taught for so long that they are virtues, partly because of a strongly entrenched self–discipline or habit, we become obtuse to the fact that we *have* carried them to excess. Sometimes, in fact, entire lifetimes must pass before the sin of our virtue carried to excess becomes apparent to us.

Independence, for example, is commonly regarded as a desirable state of being and a goal to be achieved by all self-respecting countries and individuals. To be "self-determined" is one of the aims of Scientologists and, in the sense in which they are using it, there is no doubt that theirs is a valid concept. But too much independence and too much self-determinism can be just as bad as too much dependence or other—determinism—especially if selfishness or the ego becomes involved.

An interesting case in point is that of a woman whose past-life history includes two experiences in which the attitude of independence became more and more deeply ingrained. The first one was in England at the time of Cromwell when she was a spinster schoolteacher; the second, and more recent, was in Jamestown and Williamsburg when, again as a woman, she was "among those that helped in establishing the tenets of self-government." Cayce goes on to say that the entity "gained in the experience—gained until there arose self-indulgence in the activity. . . and the feeling that there should be the rule of self irrespective of another."

He then comments that wherever there is individual activity there must also be thought taken of the other people involved, and continues by saying: "In the present we find an influence of independency in this entity, and the tendency for this to make for experiences of consternation and disturbances. *For one may become too independent as well as too dependent upon others, situations, conditions—whether these pertain to the material, the mental, or the spiritual.*"

The woman acknowledged to the present writer that this was one of the most revealing and helpful sentences of the entire reading; that for the first time she became aware of this tendency within herself and of the fact that it was this, in fact, that had alienated people from her, both in conversation and in several basic life situations.

She began to correct it, making an almost painful effort to accept favors where before she had refused them, or to receive assistance in situations where before she had regarded it as a point of honor to be sternly self-sufficient. Her relations with people and especially with men became much more easy and happy as a result.

Another interesting case is that of a man who once must have ardently desired complete independence of action—and had achieved it, as an Egyptian ruler of almost unlimited power. He had absolute control not only over his subjects but also over the spiritual leaders of the time. The total independence which becomes the lot of the rich and the powerful was his; but, as so often happens, it was abused, which is to say, it was used by the ego rather than impersonally.

In the present lifetime this same entity is the director of a benevolent organization which is not privately endowed and which must rely on the good will, the financial donations, and the personal help of many persons all over the country. He finds himself in the situation of having to avail himself of volunteer help whenever he can, without offending by refusal those who are willing but inept; having to accept hospitality and assistance from some who might wish to dictate policies or procedure; and adjust the demands of many varying personalities to the best needs of the organization as a whole. His position, in short, despite the fact that he is a leader in a position of authority, is largely one of dependence; it requires the utmost of diplomacy and tact and the selfless consideration of the long-range interests of many other people besides himself.

Life has placed him in an inescapable position where he must be dependent upon some of those same people whom he "pushed around," as the expressive colloquialism has it, in the past. In this way a just balance between independence and dependence is gradually being achieved.

To be sure, all of us need ultimately to become self-sufficient and complete within ourselves—having the full attributes of God and needing nothing outside ourselves.* But as long as we are in human form it is well to remember that mutual interdependence is a fact of nature, the honest and willing acknowledgment of which is the only sensible and gracious approach. Trees breathe in the noxious atmosphere that we breathe out; for our very breathing the trees and we are mutually inter-

---

*There is one school of thought that holds, on the other hand, that even God Himself felt the need of His creation. This is disputed by those who maintain that if God were perfect He could not feel the need of anything . . .

dependent. The whole earth planet exhibits this same kind of mutual interaction and usefulness; and so, no doubt, does the entire cosmos. We are members of one another, as Paul puts it; the eyes may perform their seeing with beautiful rectitude and independence; but is it only a seeming independence, because without the mouth and the stomach they could not function at all. In the same way do human occupations and talents supplement each other; and at one point or another all of us must acknowledge our dependence, even as instruments in a great symphonic orchestra.

Balance in the sense of equipoise, then, is necessary between too great independence and too great dependence. It is necessary, in fact, between any of the opposite polarities of quality, between which we must walk as warily as a tightrope walker upon his high-stretched rope.

"Do not be over-democratic; neither too self-sufficient," Cayce counsels one individual. "There is a medium ground on which all may meet."

To another he says: "Never think too highly of yourself, and never belittle yourself too much."

Even selflessness, it seems, can be overdone. Selflessness, like independence, is generally regarded as a virtue to be striven for—especially among those who are spiritually rather than psychologically oriented. In fact, to become selfless is one of the principal messages of the Cayce readings. So it is almost surprising to find that Cayce himself remarking in a number of instances that selflessness can be excessive. An examination of some of these cases shows that there are varying psychological reasons for this.

In one case, a woman was told that in a past life she was the wife of a distinguished man whom everybody praised and admired; her own gifts and influence went largely unappreciated. This caused in her a sense of self-belittlement which persisted into the present. "This is what must be overcome," Cayce says. "For while selflessness is the law, to belittle oneself is actually a form of selfishness, and not selflessness."

In another similar case the danger of the tendency for self-belittlement is explained more explicitly. "You are one," he tells the woman, "that is prone to belittle its own abilities—and this is seldom found. But there should be a greater desire in you for the expression of yourself and your undertakings and your knowledge. True, one must become selfless; but to have knowledge and withhold it from others is not always best."

It becomes clear from cases like this that the basic attitude of humility and selflessness which could be formulated by the phrase *I am not important* can lead to negativity—and hence to sins of omission, to the failure to make a positive contribution to the lives of others when one has the knowledge and the insight to do so. This may be related to the fear of being rejected or the fear of not being highly thought of; and whatever is tinged with fear shows the absence of love. Hence such a selflessness is not perfect.

A totally different picture is found in the case of a woman osteopath who asked at the end of her reading: "How may I be of more service to my patients and human beings in general?"

Cayce's answer ran as follows:

"This may not sound just right. It may sound like a selfish approach. But when the abilities and activities of this entity are deeply considered, this counsel will be seen to be proper. For in all spiritual activities, there must be first the individual and then the group. There must be first service *to oneself*; then there is a better flow of the coordinating activities of life and vitality, and thus a better fitting of the body for service to patients and mankind in general."

In this case the formulation of selflessness, *I am not important,* had led in turn to the formulation, *I must help others, not myself.* But neglect of oneself can lead not only to diminished vitality and helpfulness to others, but also to the thwarting of one's own evolution. To neglect oneself and one's own progress in the name of helping others may thus be a dodging of responsibility; a form of inertia, perhaps. Or it may be related to neurotic compulsions, guilt feelings, or overcompensation of one kind or another.

To be self-regarding, it seems, is just as important as to be other—regarding; an excess in either direction may be symptomatic of other defects of character, and may lead to serious imbalances that will require painful correction sooner or later in the soul's long education.

# 16

# Balance: The Triangle

*Life is lived not only on the biological level, but also on the emotional and the men-*tal. And it seems that frequently the laws that are applicable to one level of being are also applicable to the others.

We know, for example, that a balanced diet is important. And, as we have already noted, balance in this sense refers to a proportionate distribution of proper food energies to the various requirements of the body. The concept would seem to apply to the psychological level as well. A healthy life is possible only when there is an appropriate distribution of energies to all the various departments of living.

"Remember," Cayce said, "that all work and no play will make just as dull a boy as all play and no work. Eventually you will be worthless to yourself and to others, and to that which you desire to accomplish."

"It is best," he continued, "that every individual should budget his time. Set aside so much time for study, so much for relaxation, so much for physical activity, so much for social activity. And while it is not meant that you should do this merely as a matter of rote, it *is* meant that each of the changes and each of these activities will make for the creating of a better *balance."*

In another reading he spoke in the same vein: "There must be a certain amount of recreation, a certain amount of rest. There are physical, mental, and spiritual necessities."

Even Jesus, Cayce pointed out, lived a balanced life. "Take time to be holy," he said, "but take time to play also. Take time to rest, time to recuperate; for even the Master took time to rest, took time to be apart from others, took time to meditate and pray, took time to attend a wedding."

It is interesting in this connection to note that Cayce also insisted that humor is an important part of the balanced personality, and he surprises us by remarking that Jesus Himself had a sense of humor. This, along with the description Cayce gives us of Jesus' brothers and sisters, His membership in the Essene brotherhood, and His studies in Persia and India,* is something of which we find no mention in our present version of the Bible; though—as one reflects upon it—it seems much more plausible that one so spiritually liberated and in possession of such extraordinary mastery over matter *should* have a sense of humor rather than not. Spirituality and humor are both possible only where there is detachment from the tyranny of matter.

In any case, most healthy-minded psychologists would agree that humor is the visible token of a free-flowing and well-balanced personality. Cayce stressed the point frequently, and urged the cultivation of humor as a spiritual gift.

A person suffering from a serious psychoneurosis asked in a reading how he could overcome his fear. Cayce answered: "By seeing the ridicu-

---

*Many times the Cayce clairvoyance gave information on historical events and personages which went beyond, or even contrary to, existing records; but as any student of history or general semantics knows, incomplete and distorted accounts are the rule rather than the exception in the history of human reporting. Only the future discovery of other written records, or the independent concurrence of other clairvoyants, can establish the accuracy or inaccuracy of what Cayce said with regard to the little-known portions of Jesus' life.

lous side of every experience. By knowing and believing in the Lord; for without that consciousness of the indwelling of the Lord, little may ever be accomplished." Here, as elsewhere, humor and spirituality are placed side by side.

Two persons who had a tendency to take life too seriously were given substantially the same advice. One was told: "This entity has the tendency of always seeing the dark side. It would be very well for him to cultivate humor and wit and the ability to see the ridiculous. For know that life, the body, the mind, are as much or more for enjoyment. Cultivate cheerfulness. You desire to bring it into the experience of others. Then it must be in your own daily experience also. See the joyfulness of the Master of men! See the joyfulness of those who were persecuted for His sake—as Stephen, Paul, Peter, and the others! All of these showed their joy in the Lord; and over and over again it is indicated that His joy makes for peace and harmony in your experience."

And to the other he said: "Hold, then, to the ability to be witty. Stop being so serious. Laugh it off. He did—even on the cross in Calvary!"

The sense of joyousness, playfulness, exuberance, of being equal to all the contingencies of life, is an essential part of the healthy and balanced individual. It is found in every normal young creature, in kittens and puppies and baby bears as well as in a human child, who has normal health and a normal sense of love and security. It is lost by those who are in some way insecure or who fear, hate, or grieve. It is absent, in short, only where there is a preponderance of negative, constrictive emotions—against which Christ surely spoke clearly enough.

This emphasis on humor as being consistent with, and even indicative of, true spirituality is one point at which Cayce departs from traditional churchly attitudes. There is another point where he departs not only from the traditional religious but also from the traditional psychiatric approach. And this is in his concept of man as a threefold being, composed of body, mind, and soul. Though soul is in a sense primary, nonetheless these three parts are, on this plane of existence, of equal importance.

This is a radical departure from the ordinary psychological or psychiatric viewpoint, because the soul has long since been outlawed from respectable scientific thinking. Except in the approach of Jung, the majority of modern psychologists and psychoanalysts would not be caught dead talking about a soul—and would certainly be embarrassed to be caught dead *having* one! And it is a radical departure from the ordinary religious viewpoint because, although most religious groups acknowledge the existence and reality of the body, most of them also have a deep-rooted feeling of guilt and shame about it. They might concede its importance as a factor to be reckoned with, and they might provide with true Christian charity for its needs of food, clothing, and shelter; but many of them would feel it unseemly to regard it as being of equal importance to the soul.

But Cayce is unequivocal in his insistence that the body is equally as important as the soul. This viewpoint is not possible—indeed, would be dangerously heretical—in a religion that regards spirit and matter to be warring and irreconcilable opposites; but Cayce often expressed the self-same viewpoint with regard to the nature of matter as that arrived at by contemporary physicists. As early as 1926 he said: *"For all should realize that matter in any form is of the spirit."*

This is all quite consonant with the conception we have developed in previous chapters—namely that the body is at the same time a partial projection of the soul (at a lower degree of density, so to speak) and its mirror—like instrumentality. *To ignore or in any way disparage the body, then, would be to fail actually, in one's obligation to the soul itself.*

Moreover, Cayce's philosophy of Oneness—the Oneness of all force, the Oneness of truth, the Oneness of all peoples—applies even here. He does not regard the body, mind, and soul as separate entities, but as aspects merely of the same thing. "Do this. . . in mind, in body, and in spirit," he concludes one little sermon on the balanced life, "for these three are *one*—ever one!"

He frequently told people that their first step towards living a better life was to formulate their ideals. But their ideals were not merely to be spiritual ones; they were to be physical and mental ones as well. "Write them down on paper!" he often said. "Make three columns: Physical, Mental, and Spiritual . . . Know that each phase of your experience—body, mind, and soul—needs to be cultivated. You have to feed the physical body, don't you? Then feed your mind, too. Have a regular diet for your spirit—and remember, you'll need as many vitamins for the spirit as you will for the body!" The blueprint for a truly healthy and fulfilled life, obviously, in the Cayce conception at least, must include these three parts in equal measure.

How often people fall short of one or another of these aspects of the perfect pattern becomes apparent in many of the Cayce readings. In case after case one finds him contemplating a life and making suggestions for its improvement—almost like an art instructor who, going from easel to easel in his life class, sees how his students have distorted the fine proportions of the model; a foreshortened leg on this canvas, an oversized hand on another, a badly drawn line of the clavicle on still another. With a quick light touch of his charcoal, he tries to show each student how best to bring the figure back into proportion.

To many people he found it necessary to point out the need for a greater balance between thought and action, between study and application. "It is just as great a sin to overeat as to overdrink," he told one individual; "to over-*think* as to over-act!"

"Don't study so much," he told another, "but *apply* more of what you know. You'll get a lot more out of it, and it will do others more good, too . . . In doing comes understanding. Be ye a doer, not a hearer only!"

Again and again he pointed out to intellectuals their fatal tendency to live too much in the ivory towers of the mind, without applying their knowledge to their own bodies and lives, or in the workshops of the world. But other persons have their imbalances also.

"If you become too health conscious," he told one ardent physical culturist, "or so addicted to this routine or that, it will be just as serious as if you did little or nothing about your health!"

And there were other individuals who apparently relied too much on their intuition or their "inner guidance"—soul qualities, presumably—who were told in no uncertain terms that they ought to read and study more along comparative lines.

Not only did Cayce find imbalances with regard to the three major areas of being—body, mind, and soul—but he also found imbalances within the imbalances.

Here, for example, is a person who is unselfish (which is a soul quality, of love) with respect to his family, but very selfish with respect to all other human beings; here is another who is very patient (another soul quality) with respect to the details of wood carving, but very impatient with respect to the failings of other people. Here is one who is brilliant (a mind quality) with respect to inorganic chemistry, and very stupid with regard to the social amenities and the way to raise a child. Here is one with the capacity for intense application (which is will) to the problems of mechanics, and no capacity whatsoever for willing an abstinence from drink and from food.

All these inequalities, with regard to different spheres of activity, must be equalized; and the circumstances and relationships of many lifetimes serve to bring about that equalization.

The Young Men's Christian Association has for many years had as its emblem an equilateral triangle. Its three equal sides symbolize their equal cultivation of the needs of body, mind, and spirit.

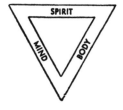

Though Cayce himself never actually spoke of a triangle in this manner, we can in all probability be faithful both to the letter and the spirit of his conception if we adapt the triangle as a means of visually clarifying it. Thinking in geometrical terms for psychological purposes is more Pythagorean than it is modern, to be sure, but a return to this type of thinking may prove fruitful. Certainly it can help systematize our thinking in an easily rememberable way.

Before going any further, however, it might be well to observe in passing that the words "spirit" and "soul" present something of a semantic problem. They are generally used interchangeably, but many religionists and occultists would insist that there is a difference between them. Cayce regarded the soul as "a part, a shadow of the real spiritual self"; but although on several occasions he made this technical distinction when asked about it, he more often than not seemed to use the terms more loosely and in an interchangeable way. In any case, we will for the sake of simplicity proceed with our argument using the word "soul" rather than the word "spirit."

Returning now (like Archimedes during the invasion of Syracuse) to our triangles, we will find that we can, thinking in geometrical terms, easily visualize the imbalance that results when an individual has *not* attached equal importance to these three departments of his being, or when he has given body or mind the place of ascendency rather than soul. The ideal or perfect triangle can be regarded as equi-sided and equi-angled. But if a person has developed his mind at the expense of his soul and his body, we can clearly see the result in a distorted triangle as represented below:

This kind of triangle would picture the imbalanced condition of many college professors, Ph.D.'s, engineers, psychologists, psychiatrists, physicists, literary critics, and intellectuals generally.

A person who, on the other hand, had paid exaggerated attention to his body would have his triangle stretched out of shape in the other direction:

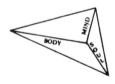

Here we have the triangulated image of many professional athletes and dancers, gourmets, sensualists, hedonists, merchants, businessmen, and movie stars.

Whereas a person who had paid excessive attention to his soul (rare in our country) would present an equally unedifying triangular picture:

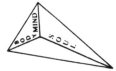

This kind of triangle would represent such persons as the mystic, the religious devotee, and perhaps certain kinds of artists.

Not only do certain occupational groups, or certain types of people have these imbalances, but certain races and nations, it would seem, tend to have them also. It is dangerous, of course, to generalize; generalizations have a tendency to be fallible. But there does seem to be some validity, at least, in the notion that India has, in past centuries, become disproportionate in its emphasis upon soul and its neglect of body—its neglect of the material world in general. On the other hand, the United States of America by and large has tended to become disproportionate in its emphasis upon body, upon material devices and physical things, with a corresponding underdevelopment of soul.

George Bernard Shaw was one of the several great thinkers who observed this tendency. He suggested that a marriage of East and West, a synthesis of both their anti-polar emphases, would result in a healthier East, a healthier West, and a healthier world.

It would be difficult to point to a nation in which there has been an analogous disproportion with regard to the mind. Perhaps the white race as a whole could be regarded as an example of this overemphasis. Certainly the white race has made the greatest technological advances of any contemporary race at least; and it takes great pride in its accomplishments and its mental capacities. The I.Q. (intelligence quotient) is one of its shibboleths of superiority, and it tends to regard with complacent superiority any race whose I.Q. presumably does not equal its own.

Such an assumption of superiority merely on the basis of mind superiority is clearly seen to be fallacious when one thinks in terms of our triplicity of being. Other races may be less mentally acute, but they may be more spiritually mature (as the Hindus), more deeply founded in their love nature (as the Mexicans), or more beautiful and healthy on the physical level (as the Balinese).

From the point of view of triplicity, in fact, it becomes clear that a truly superior race is not yet among us on this planet. Only a race that is beautiful and perfect in body, mind, and soul could be regarded as superior; and one possibility that suggests itself is that it may be through a *fusion* of existing races that the imbalances of each will be canceled out, and the strengths of each forged into one superb type.

If we give a backward glance at the symbols of the early Gnostics we find, in connection with triplicity, a very significant thing. We find that God was represented by these early philosophers geometrically, by an equilateral triangle—the three points (or perhaps the sides) of the triangle indicating God's three aspects of Intelligence, Love, and Power (or Will).

That God is all-intelligent, all-loving, and all-powerful is not alien to Christian thinking; and though Christians have not usually thought in terms of triangles,* they *have* thought in terms of a trinity. The Father, Son, and Holy Ghost trinity, however, does not seem as significant or as useful, psychologically speaking, as the Intelligence, Love, and Power trinity. For if we analyze these more closely we see that intelligence equates itself with mind; love equates itself with soul; and power (or will or energy) could well equate itself with body.

It must be remembered that on the human level we always have a semantic problem. Lao Tse puts it very well when he says: "Existence is beyond the power of words to define: Terms may be used, but none of them are absolute. . . :" Actually, the threefold division of man's being into body, mind, and soul probably includes a number of aspects to which we give different names at our level of perception, but which are actually intimately related.

In the phenomenon of body, for example, can be included a cluster of aspects: energy, power, dexterity, application, practicality, will. In mind can be included many facets also: inventiveness, ingenuity, intellectual perception, comparison, knowledge. Soul can include the things we call

---

*In one case at least they have, however. The Trappist monks, who are dedicated to a life of absolute silence, communicate with each other when necessary by symbols made with the hands; their symbol for God is made by forming the thumb and forefinger of both hands into a triangle.

love, warmth, enthusiasm, reverence, devotion, emotion, perhaps even intuition, since love leads to identification with the loved one and hence to immediate knowing without intellectual processes. So the threefold division of man's being may well be broader, subtler, and more psychologically valid than we might at first glance think. What is more, it gives us a rational correspondence to the Divine Nature that helps to bring psychology and religion intimately and intelligibly to terms.

Pursuing this line of thought still further, we are led to still further clarifications. Christ told us that we should become perfect, even as our Father which is in heaven is perfect. If we grasp the import of this sentence fully and realistically, we will see then that to be truly perfect is to be like God, all-knowing, all-loving, and all-powerful, or perfect with respect to the mind, to the soul, and to the body. It is as if we were all miniature triangles—distorted and muddy little triangles—and we need to clean out the mud and let the light shine through. We also need to bring into equivalence each side and each one of the three attributes of God.

It would mean having, ultimately, the capacity to be and to act with excellence, with regard to everything. It would mean having perfect love, not only with regard to human beings, but also with regard to animals and flowers and minerals; not only with regard to cherished ideas, but also with regard to tiny creatures. It would mean having perfect intelligence (perhaps translucence would be the more accurate term) with regard to every possible area of thought, and perfect power with regard to every possible area of acting. It would mean dwelling, as it were, in the center of the triangle and flowing energies equally to all three points.

And, since every equilateral triangle can be circumscribed by a circle and by a sphere, we would find ourselves then at the center of a circle and of a sphere (the perfect figure, according to ancient philosophers). And suddenly it becomes clear that to become Sons of God is also to become Suns of God—the light of the sun being intelligence, its warmth being love, and its energy being will or power—and the ancient Egyptian symbol of the sun as an object of reverence seems far less "pagan," far more alive with pregnant and urgent meaning than we might at first glance assume.

# 17

# Balance: The Pendulum

*There would seem to be two major determinants in our destiny. One is our own* desire. The other is the action of karma.

Inasmuch as freedom of will was given us from the very beginning, according to Cayce, our desire could have unlimited fulfillment were it not for the fact that it has become selfish and separative; it has gone contrary to the universal good or to the law of universal love. Karma comes into play, then, only because we have not used our freedom of will, or desire, wisely. Thus karma is, as it were, merely the safety device of the machinery. Whenever any of us knows the frustration of desire, or the hampering of our freedom of will, it is transparently indicative that the desire or the freedom, for one reason or another, needed chastening, correction, or purification.

Both of these two factors, desire and karma, seem to operate at times by a kind of pendulum action; and in both cases the swing of the pendulum seems to have as its ultimate purpose a balancing or equipoise between and above two opposite states of limited being.

In a very interesting passage of the tenth book of *The Republic*, Plato describes certain Greek heroes who, after being judged by the gods for their deeds in life, are allowed to choose their bodies for their next incarnation on earth.

"Most curious was the spectacle," relates the man who observed the scene, "sad and laughable and strange; for the choice of the souls was in most cases based on their own experiences of a previous life." He goes on to tell how the soul who had been Orpheus chose the "life of a swan, out of enmity to the race of women—hating to be born of a woman because they had been his murderers." Ajax chose the life of a lion—refusing to be a man again because of the injustice that men had done him. Agamemnon chose the life of an eagle; like Ajax, he hated human nature because of his sufferings at human hands.

As for Odysseus, Plato had this to say: "Now the recollection of former toils had disenchanted him of ambition, and he went about for a considerable time in search of the life of a private man who has no care. He had some difficulty in finding this, which was lying about and had been neglected by everyone else; and when he saw it he said that he would have done the same had his lot been first instead of last, and that he was delighted to have it."

In all of these instances we have beautifully illustrated for us the same basic psychological operation: the revulsion from a certain area of experience and the decision to have no more part of it. In the cases of Orpheus, Ajax, and Agamemnon, who chose incarnation as a swan, a lion, and an eagle respectively, we may perhaps feel that this is to be interpreted allegorically. But in the case of Odysseus, there is no allegory about it: he is disenchanted with ambition, and he determines *to live the life of a private man who has no cares.*

Decisions like this one—leading an individual from one type of life to its diametric opposite—are probably fairly common in cases where great suffering or disillusionment has been part of the experience. We can well imagine persons who vow *never* to marry again, or never to be alone; never to have children again, or never to be childless; never to have a position of prominence again, or never again to be obscure.

As a matter of fact, we see many cases of this type in the Cayce readings. "I will *never* get involved emotionally with someone again," an entity vowed in Atlantis; and for at least three succeeding lifetimes it has lived solitary and unmarried lives, true to its decision. In India, centuries ago, a man was among the warriors who descended into the valley, killed the men, and took the women prisoners. "And from that experience of many women," Cayce tells him, "the entity may be called a one-woman man now, because the experiences were sad in the latter portion of that period. "

In England, during the struggle "between royalty and the common people," a certain entity gave much of itself for the development of others. But towards the end of its life it discovered that these efforts were largely to no purpose and unappreciated, "Hence in the present, we have the great satisfaction it takes in getting just what it wants most for itself." A Christian in early Rome, persecuted in mind and in body, suffered so deeply for following its spiritual principles that in the following incarnation it gave itself entirely to a life of material satisfactions.

In all of these cases—from deep emotional involvement to *no* emotional involvements; from many women to one woman; from great altruism to great self-centeredness; from a life of spirituality to a life of materiality—we see the pendulum swing of desire and of choice.

Sometimes one or the other of the lateral swings of the pendulum is closer to the side of wisdom and the angels—but the very fact that in the above cases there was a revulsion to the opposite extreme indicates some kind of ego involvement and spiritual deficiency or weakness.

Because of our particular cultural scale of values for one thing, and also because of certain abstract considerations, most of us would be inclined to think that to be a one-woman man is far more ideal a practice than to be a many-women man; and yet even faithfulness to one woman could conceivably have its origin more in fear and insecurity than in a fully conscious and integrated love, and thus be more neurotic than otherwise. In such a case there could be another rebound to the opposite extreme of an experience with many women; and so forth and so on until such time as the true inner equipoise was reached with regard to all women, and perhaps reunion with the true "soul mate," if there be such a thing, was achieved.

The pendulum or rebound principle in human choice is very interesting, psychologically speaking; it is a factor that helps to clarify much in the subtle area of human temperament. Perhaps many psychological "blocks," "compulsions," or "fixations" are related to some intensely made decision—made one or two or many lives ago—never to be or to do such and such a thing again. If the point of origin of such decisions can be reached, and the mistaken evaluation dissolved, then a great stride forward in personality transformation can take place.* Ultimately, the result of these rebounds is that the soul not only becomes free of rigidity and narrowly fixed points of view, but also achieves the great positive qualities of flexibility and discrimination.

But it is the pendulum principle in connection with karma that clarifies much in the grosser areas of human destiny. In the realm of choice, the pendulum principle has to do primarily with the inner world. But in the realm of karma, the pendulum principle represents the equilibrating action of the universe itself, which in its determination to have balance establishes those outer circumstances which *seem* to be "circumstances beyond our control" and which constrict and frustrate us in order to educate us.

In many cases in the Cayce files the karmic pendulum is apparent, but perhaps the most clear-cut example of it is to be seen in the case of a girl born in Norfolk, Virginia, who throughout her childhood and adolescence suffered keenly from an inferiority complex because of her slight stature and her constantly ailing health. Her older sister, born ten months earlier than she, had the advantage not only of being of normal size, but also of being prettier and the pet of their widowed mother.

Here we have a classic case of the inferiority complex. At one level, at least, its origin is directly traceable to biological causes. The mother, bearing the second child only ten months after the first,

---

*The general semantics principle of Non-Allness can be one very useful tool in the dissolution of such absolute postulates. See Kenneth S. Keyes, Jr., *How to Develop Your Thinking Ability* (New York: McGraw-Hill Book Co., Inc., 1950) and Irving J. Lee, *Language Habits in Human Affairs* (New York: Harper & Brothers, 1941)

was depleted in energy and lacking in mineral elements; the second child began life even in the womb with the handicap of insufficiency.

But if we are unsatisfied by the notion that psychic facts can be entirely explained in terms of biological origins, we become desirous of knowing deeper causes—and such deeper causes, psychic in nature, are provided for us by the Cayce clairvoyance.

The Cayce reading begins, as usual, with a quick backward recapitulation of the individual's life—a kind of age-regression survey—and then starts the reading proper by saying, "In giving the interpretation of the records as we find them here, we find that there is much from which to choose . . . We choose the following with the desire that this may be a helpful experience for the entity, enabling it to know itself better and to analyze the purposes for which it chose the present environment."

It proceeds to give an accurate characterization of the girl, and then launches into her previous life history, going from the most recent previous life in early Williamsburg to her most distant one in ancient Egypt.

It is in the third life back, in Palestine at the time of Christ, that we observe something very significant: namely that the entity, then again a woman, was delicate in body and slight in build . . . She suffered much physically, the reading says, and felt deeply the "desire for strength and power and the physical ability to meet emergencies." She prayed often for a strong physical body and there was within her "that determination which brought at last the experience of the stalwart Bruce. . . ."

The stalwart Bruce was the entity's next earth experience when as a man—and what a man! exclaims the reading—the entity's intense desire and lifelong prayers for a strong body were finally fulfilled. And it would seem that the entity, as Bruce, used its strength and height well, dedicating itself to a cause and a spiritual ideal, and becoming a leader in the Crusades.

In the following life we find the entity again as a woman—a beautiful woman, the wife of a man who came from England and who had a position of authority in Williamsburg. And in this position, the entity "lorded itself over others," the reading says, becoming complacent in her beauty, snobbish, haughty, and condescending.

Piecing together this analysis with indications elsewhere that self-aggrandizing and lording it over others because of superior strength or beauty can result in future incarnations in a body abnormally short or abnormally tall, we come to the conclusion that we have before us a singularly interesting pattern.

In outline form, the pattern is this:

> A soul finds itself in a small, frail body. (This as a result of an unknown previous karmic cause.)
> It ardently desires and prays for strength.
> It finds itself next in a strong body.
> It uses the strength well, in service of an unselfish ideal.
> It finds itself again (as a reward, so to speak) in a strong, beautiful body.
> It exploits its strength and beauty in pride, and in lording it over others.
> So once again it finds itself in a small, frail body.

There are a number of interesting aspects in this case history. For one thing, it demonstrates once again the phenomenon which we have already examined in an earlier chapter: namely, the significance of the body as an *indicator* of the psyche and of various areas of the unconscious. For another thing, it shows how *ego* becomes the villain, as it were, in the drama of life. When service to an ideal was paramount in the entity's mind, its body remained proportionate and of normal stature. When thoughts of ego–importance predominated, a reduction of stature and personal beauty resulted. The body became the arena of these conflicting forces within her, and also the place of redemption.

A third thing demonstrated by this case is the force of desire and of prayer. Even if we put prayer into the category merely of a thought persistently held, a desire consistently dwelt upon, and disregard any possibility of some Being "granting" the prayer, we can see how ultimately the thought externalized itself into reality. Perhaps all strongly held desires and prayers are similarly externalized, even though there may be, as here, a considerable lag of time.

But perhaps what is most interesting in this case is the pendulum movement involved—a movement which is seen so frequently in other cases in the Cayce files as to suggest a basic pattern of destiny which can be mathematically diagramed.

Let us consider first an imaginary case before we diagram the case of the girl from Norfolk.

DIAGRAM 1

Let us take OZ as our base line (in Diagram 1), letting O represent our Source or the Godhead; and letting Z represent an individual who is on the path of return to that Source.

Ideally, the path of return would be to remain on that line or beam, proceeding slowly but surely on a straight and narrow path of light.

But actually the path of return does not usually seem to be so direct and simple.

Z is an innocent soul, newly minted, so to speak, ignorant of his divine nature.

He begins to identify himself with the animal body in which he finds himself; and, feeling a deep instinctive assurance of power, it seems only right and proper to him that he should further his own animal welfare, his own self-interest, even if it involves the murder of another.

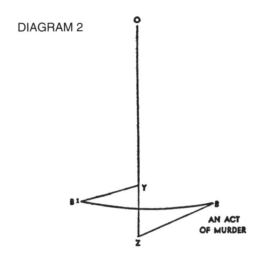

DIAGRAM 2

AN ACT
OF MURDER

We see him, then, depart from the divine path (the path from Z to O) to commit a cruel murder. (Point B in Diagram 2.)

But by the law of equilibrium which governs the universe, this act must be exactly compensated for.

Divine justice may not operate immediately; it may not be until one lifetime or several lifetimes later that entity Z experiences the suffering of a cruel murder (at B¹), either his own or that of one whom he loves dearly. In this way he is taught the lesson: *Thou shalt not kill!*

At Y the entity has been brought, through his suffering, to the awareness of what is right action; he has been brought back on the narrow beam of light. He knows it is wrong to kill.

But the soul forgets; or he may not have learned his lesson completely. He may not commit murder again, but he may commit what amounts to murder on the psychological level: he may cruelly defame another's character in order to serve his own self-interest.

Once again we see the evil, separative act at C; once again the pendulum swings to C¹, where he experiences in a later life an exact recompense for what he did to others in having someone else defame *his* character; once again the suffering which leads to the deep inner awareness: *Thou shalt not bear false witness!* (Diagram 3.)

DIAGRAM 3

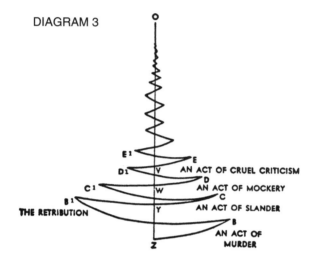

And so the progress of the soul goes—not a straight line but a zigzag one, like that of a drunkard weaving his way home; till finally the pendulum swings of evil action and painful reaction become less and less, and the soul goes directly and serenely, like the prodigal son, back to his Father and his Home.

All karmic action, in its retributive or corrective aspect, seems to follow this general pattern.

When one considers then how many fields of action there are, and how many "qualities," as we call them, need to be learned by the soul, one begins to get a glimpse of the complexity of the human psyche and the intricacy of the events that make up its "fate." Each person's path through life can be visualized on such an axis as this; and all of his ungodlike actions can be visualized as pendulum swings away from the axis-projecting in every direction, and being compensated for with precise mathematical pendulum action. There are a thousand facets to be perfected; a thousand disequilibriums to be made right.

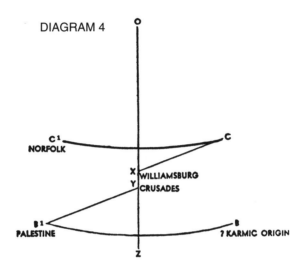

Coming back now to the case of the Norfolk girl whose inferiority feelings because of her small body colored her whole psychic life, we find that the case plots itself exactly upon this diagram.

We find her, in Palestine, on the negative side of the axis. We are not told what brought her there; we can infer a karmic cause generated in a previous life. (Diagram 4.)

Suffering led her to strong desire and prayer; together these three forces brought her in the following life to a male body, strong and stalwart. (To be strong and beautiful is our divine prerogative; it is to be on the beam of light.) Dedicated service to a cause kept the soul advancing on the beam upwards; in the following life it was born again with strength and beauty. But now an insidious element enters: pride, the desire to lord it over others. And the acts performed under the impetus of this led to karmic consequence—a consequence which she is suffering now in the present lifetime.

Undoubtedly she yearns to have a beautiful and normal body. And undoubtedly in some future life she will have it. Once again the possession of that beautiful body will be a test.

If she will have learned by that time the lesson of non-attachment to the body, which all of us must learn, she will generate no future karma in that area at least. But if she has not learned it, then the pendulum will move again, from this side to that, back and forth, back and forth, till finally she will have learned to dwell lightly in her body, in conscious possession of it but not being possessed by it.

And in that distant time, people will see upon her face and in her body that sense of serene inward identity that makes so mysteriously beautiful those ancient stone figures that still sit looking out over Egyptian sands.

# 18

# Balance: Some Implications

*From the very beginning, we have recognized that karma (in its retributive aspect at* least) is an action and reaction, equal and opposite. All textbooks in Theosophy teach this; it is a commonplace of Hindu thought.

There are great lessons to be learned merely from this basic concept of karma. The knowledge that whatever we do comes back to us in exact measure:

1. acts as a deterrent to evil and selfish actions;

2. offers an explanation for the frustrations and agonies of life, that come to seemingly undeserving people;

3. gives a scientific rationale for the teachings of Christ and of all other great religious teachers;

4. gives us a sense of moral purpose in the universe—of order and of law.

But we are given additional insight into the matter when we realize through the Cayce readings that karma is a balancing principle, and that it operates only when a certain kind of balance in the universe has been disturbed. Where balance has not been disturbed, the soul proceeds serenely along a straight line, so to speak, upon a beam of light, without alarms or confusions or agonies.

Our understanding is also broadened and deepened by the awareness that balance can be understood in several senses, and that one of the other major senses is that of self-contained symmetry. Each of us must become a unit that is perfectly balanced *within itself*; every part of us, as in a work of art, must be proportionately developed. There are certain types of experience, then, that might come to us, not in equilibrating retribution, but as a spur and a prod, to force us to grow in an undeveloped area. "Your pain," writes Kahlil Gibran in *The Prophet*,* "is but the breaking of the shell that encloses your understanding." There are some kinds of pain apparently that might be better understood in this light rather than in the light of karma as ordinarily thought of. In this case it is only the absence of a quality that makes a suffering necessary—only an omission rather than a commission.

This knowledge provides us with a clue for self-analysis, the analysis of others, and the analysis of destiny; but more than mere analysis, it provides us with an instrument of change. And the change can help us avoid the karma that might otherwise have come to us. We have prophylactic (preventive) toothbrushes; surely we should also be able to have a prophylactic ethics and mode of conduct.

Let us review here some of the ways in which Cayce shows us that balance is important, and see how they lead directly to changed thinking and changed modes of conduct.

For one thing, we will remember that assimilations and eliminations in the body should be equal so that there may be health and youth and freedom from toxins. But this law is undoubtedly transferable to psychological levels also. If that is so, we will realize that we can receive no kindness without soon thereafter passing on a comparable kindness to someone—whether to the original giver of the kindness or to another, it

---

*New York: Alfred A. Knopf, Inc., 1923

may not much matter. We will receive no material thing, or buy no new object, without passing on some material thing to another person. We will receive no new knowledge without passing that knowledge on to another—either as knowledge or as its equivalent in usage. In short, we will permit no thing to accumulate within us and thus create an imbalance to be rectified later by pain. We will sense ourselves to be *channels*, to use one of Cayce's favorite expressions—"channels of blessings" and "channels of Christ"—channels, in any case, through which things flow; we will think of ourselves as energy distributors and transformers, rather than energy accumulators.

For another thing, we will learn to appraise ourselves critically with regard to our proportional distribution of energies. One excellent method of doing so would be to analyze, every night, the activities of the day by the criterion of balance. We will ask ourselves the questions: how have I exercised my will today? My love? My intelligence? How have I developed my body, my mind, and my soul? Have I had recreation and play as well as work? If we do this daily, we will soon see where our imbalances lie, and we will be able to correct them before they become too deeply entrenched.

For another thing, we will recall that the corrective action of karma can take place more than once, repetitiously, in a kind of diminishing pendulum action, until a lesson is fully learned; and this recollection can lead us to several important awarenesses. It can make us realize that whatever gift or endowment we have—beauty, height, eloquence, talent, wealth, fame—we have it only in custody, as it were, until such time as we have completely proved our worth to possess it always. All our gifts must become "incorruptible," so to speak. The awareness that we are on trial with whatever good fortune or bad fortune we now experience can alter our perspective upon our situation considerably, and enable us to handle it much more cleanly and dispassionately.

We learn to realize also that the soul's evolution is a long, slow growth. In India, it is traditionally thought that every soul reincarnates 840,000 times. The figure may well be too high; but on the other hand, in view of the infinite variety of human faculties and the long time it takes to perfect any single talent (such as playing the flute or the piano), to say nothing of the perfecting of all the many virtues of character, it would seem that many people, in thinking about this matter, tend to put the number of incarnations far too low.

Growth is not merely a question of learning new virtues or talents—learning them on a clean slate or a blank sheet of paper, so to speak. It is frequently a question of *erasing* a bad mode of action or a distorted habit of thinking and feeling. To "erase," as an analogy, is appropriate enough, but it falls far short of conveying the actual difficulties involved. A way of thinking or acting is probably an *energy pattern*—a characteristic mode of vibration in the very brain itself, with its own dynamic will to live and its own centrifugal power.

To bring a halt to these energy patterns and then change them is undoubtedly a task of great magnitude and one that must take a great deal of time. Anyone who has ever tried to break any deep-seated habit knows the practical difficulties involved. The nerve paths are so deeply channelized that it takes tremendous will power and the uplifting impact of some tremendous new idea to make possible a change in channelization.

And so to find that there can be a certain repetitiousness in the soul's history should not dismay or discourage us too much. It is not repetitiousness in Nietzsche's sense of "eternal recurrence": it is not an exact recurrence, throughout eternity. This would be too horrible to contemplate—and would, moreover, be utterly without meaning. But it is repetitiousness in the sense of the recurrence of the same kind of experience to the same soul *provided* he did not fully learn the lesson the first time, and *until* such time as he has completely learned the lesson and altered his consciousness. "So long as our will is the same, our world can be no other than it is," Schopenhauer remarked, wisely.

Dr. Fred Reinhold* has observed this same repetitiousness in his patients who were age-regressed to past lives either through hypnosis or through the use of carbon dioxide. For example, a woman patient of his who had suffered violence from men in the present lifetime seemed to show a pattern of experiencing violence from men in several previous

---

*A psychologist in Hollywood. California.

lifetimes also. Whether this was karmic in the strict sense of the term or whether it stemmed from a deep-lying and persistent masochistic need within herself, Dr. Reinhold would not say. But of one thing he was convinced, and that is that the lessons of life are not always learned as quickly and finally as a superficial acquaintance with karma and reincarnation would lead one to believe.

The same conclusion is warranted by a close study of the Cayce readings also, wherein in a given person's past-life history we see much variety but we also see persistent types of experience in some area peculiar to that particular entity. In the case of the Norfolk girl, for example, the repetitiousness was in the area of stature and of pride. In other cases it was in the area of sex, or of monkish tendencies for seclusion, or of stubbornness, or of violence. Apparently a soul lesson is not learned quickly and easily and once for all time.

That repetition is a law of learning is an axiom of educational psychology. There is no reason why it should not also be an axiom in the educational psychology of the universe.

If we reflect deeply upon this matter, also, we will see how much vanity there may be in thinking, as some people do, "I feel this is my last life on earth . . . "

This statement must be carefully distinguished from another one, which one hears with almost equal frequency, namely: "I don't *want* to come back to earth again. The desire not to return to earth can arise from a weariness of life, a sense of defeat, or a feeling that the things one suffers in life far outweigh its pleasures. This sentiment is understandable, and forgivable, provided that the individual does not thereby conclude that this proves that he will not return again. Schoolchildren are not allowed to decide for themselves that they will not return to school; they still have too much to learn. Similarly we, in the rudimentary grades of school in which we find ourselves, could hardly be allowed to decide for ourselves that we are not going to come back.

In one respect this statement is comparable, perhaps, to people saying after too much Thanksgiving dinner, "I don't want to eat again for a week!" or "I'll never *look* at turkey again!" Yet six hours later, when someone suggests a midnight snack, these same people have quite forgotten

their vow and quite lost their sense of satiety; they eat the turkey sand-
wiches. Similarly with the satiety of life, perhaps. The love of life burns
deep and strong; not even a lifetime of tragedy can fully extinguish it.

However, the statement, "I feel that this is my last life on earth" is in
quite a different category. It seems to arise partly from a great vanity,
partly from the unawareness of how much discipline, both repetitious
and varied, is required to produce a fully perfect soul, and partly from
having mistakenly identified the recognition of virtue with the possession thereof.

It is not enough to have read (or even written) a few books on mys-
ticism, meditation, or reincarnation to qualify for Christhood. It is not
enough to *understand* the laws of life, to *recognize* the principles of right
living and right thinking, or to *see* the law of moral cause and effect.

These understandings and recognitions require a certain degree of
maturity, to be sure; but they reside more in the intellective part of us
than elsewhere; *they must still be translated into flesh.* They must be objectified in our bodies and in our lives. And this takes time, and effort, and
energy, and attention, and ceaseless devotion, and the tempering action
of a great variety of circumstances.

Any artist who has struggled with his medium knows the long and
arduous discipline that is required to translate even one idea to his
canvas or his stone or his paper. How much more, then, do we all have
to struggle to objectify in the living texture which is our body the concepts of reality and rightness which little by little are dawning on our
growing awareness!

Life is not to be bought cheap. The attainment of Christhood and the
perfection towards which we are all moving is not to be bought cheap
either.

"Stand erect or be made erect!" Marcus Aurelius wrote in his journal
long ago. There is great wisdom in this line, and it applies to all of us.
Aurelius may have had no knowledge of reincarnation, but he phrased
nonetheless a very great reincarnationist truth. If we take ourselves in
hand and discipline *ourselves*, we will no longer be subject to the flagel-
lating discipline of outer circumstance.

In short, if balance is the intention of the universe, whether in the sense of equipoise between opposites, or proportional distribution of energies to all parts, or an equivalence of incoming with outgoing, or an exact replacement of displaced energies, then we can more intelligently align ourselves with the universe by consciously striving for balance in all of these areas.

In modern times, perhaps no more terse and profound expression of this wisdom can be found than in the lines of Edward Carpenter (again from "The Secret of Time and Satan"):

> *Do not be dismayed because thou art yet a child of chance, and at the mercy greatly both of Nature and fate;*
> *Because if thou were not subject to chance, then wouldst thou be Master of thyself; but since thou art not yet Master of thine own passions and powers, in that degree must thou be at the mercy of some other power.*
> *And if thou choosest to call that power "Chance," well and good.*
> *It is the angel with whom thou hast to wrestle.*

# Conclusion

# 19

# The Way Out

*For us of the Western world the idea of reincarnation is new and unaccustomed; for* the Eastern world it is as old as the rising and setting of the sun, as familiar as the household doorstep.

Two ancient traditions in particular, Hinduism and Buddhism, have taught reincarnation; and there is a great deal that we can learn from both of them. Both Hinduism and Buddhism are founded on the authority of ancient books (those of Hinduism being the much more ancient of the two), and they have been subject to varying interpretations on the part of their own followers. In doctrine and in practice they have been colored by the temperament and history of the peoples who have accepted them. For these reasons we must expect that there will be many differences between the two faiths, even as regards the basic teaching of reincarnation. It is important also for us to recognize that their teachings may not be adaptable, *in toto*, by ourselves because we

have a differing temperament, different historical and religious a
cedents, and important new scientific horizons.

A study of the parallels and divergences between Hinduism and Bu
dhism can be tremendously fascinating. However, we need not conce
ourselves with such comparisons here except in one important respe
and that is their differing viewpoints on the nature and ultimate de
tiny of the soul.

The Hindus conceive of an eternal identity which they call the atman
The atman, they say, persists through a long series of lifetimes; it casts
off worn-out bodies and personalities as a body casts off worn-out
garments; and its ultimate destiny is perfection, enlightenment, and joy.

"The truly wise," Krishna says, in a famous passage in the *Bhagavadgita*,*
"mourn neither for the living nor for the dead. There was never a time
when I did not exist, nor you, nor any of these kings. Nor is there any
future in which we shall cease to be . . . Bodies are said to die, but That
which possesses the body is eternal . . . "

In striking contrast to this view is the view of the Buddhists. The
Buddhists maintain that everything in the universe is in a state of
change, including our body, our thoughts, and our emotions. What we
are pleased to call our soul is merely a conglomeration of habit patterns
and I-attachments, also subject to change. So there is really no such
thing as a permanent soul, the Buddhists say; there is only an illusory
ego which because of its desires and its attachments takes incarnation,
yielding place to another ego which in turn takes incarnation, and so
on till it is ultimately lost in the whole, without any individuality of its
own. The aim of existence is to achieve this liberation and this state of
re-absorption.

The Cayce point of view is, in this respect at least, more closely allied
to the Hindu than to the Buddhist viewpoint. Cayce, like the Hindus,
maintains that there *is* a permanent identity or self, which transcends
and outlives the transient personalities of each successive incarnation.
To this eternal identity he gives the name of "entity" or "soul-self. "

---

*Bhagavadgita, The Song of God,* translated by Swami Prabhavananda and Christopher
Isherwood (Hollywood: The Marcel Rodd Company, 1944)

ar destiny as entities is to become "companions and co-
God." This phrase would seem to indicate that, even
inally achieve perfection and oneness with God, we also
individuality until the very end of time—or at least until
time as we understand it. We become one with the ocean of
is not so much that we are lost in the ocean as that the ocean
ed into us, since we offer no further obstruction to it. "For the
of each soul is *to know itself to be itself*," Cayce says, "*yet one with that
Force called God.*"

Cayce point of view here, while different from Christian ortho-
nonetheless is much more acceptable than the Buddhistic to
ple of Christian background. This may be because our Christian tra-
on unconsciously influences us to be predisposed towards the sur-
val of our individuality. Or it may be because we are temperamentally
ery much attached to the sense of selfhood. In any case, the Cayce
point of view seems more affirmative to us of the Western world, with
our active, ambitious temperament, than the Buddhistic, which affects
many Westerners as being nihilistic. The idea of an eternal identity gives
us the reassurance that our strivings and sufferings are not useless and
in vain, and it gives us encouragement to continue to pursue all our
goals.

But whether we believe in an eternal identity or not, one fact remains—inescapable, undeniable, and pertaining to us all—the fact of
human suffering. How are we to escape it? How are we to become free
of the frustrations and the agonies that typify human life, and finally
live in freedom and joy? What is the way out?

There are various social answers to these questions. There are systems like Technocracy, Socialism, and Communism, which claim to be
able to end human misery through more equitable social and economic
arrangements. An impartial study of these systems shows that, in theory,
each of them do have many merits. Yet even assuming that these systems could do all they claim, and even granting them a maximum
length of time for the cumulative psychological effects of universal security and universal education, it is doubtful that they could really fulfill their promise. It is doubtful because human misery is not entirely of

a physical nature and universal plenty is therefore not likely to solve the human problem. As long as we have vain, arrogant, lazy, irresponsible, shallow, proud, envious, malicious, gluttonous, intemperate, intolerant, ill-tempered, cruel, vindictive, possessive, power-hungry, domineering, stupid, shortsighted, selfish, petty, rapacious, hypocritical, imperfect human beings in this world, we are going to inflict misery upon ourselves and upon each other—regardless of the fact that we might all have two cars and a station wagon in the garage, a town and a country home, a Deepfreeze and a microwave cooker, and all the food we want to eat.

Great religious teachers have always been aware of this psychological fact, and great religious systems have always been at the same time psychological systems. The world outside can never be perfect until we have perfected the world within. The way out of our misery is, in the last analysis, the way *in*, to the sources of our misery.

Christ taught this; so did Buddha; so did Krishna. It was the great mission of Edgar Cayce to restate for our age the reincarnation principle which formed the framework for the psychological systems of Buddhism and Hinduism, and at the same time reaffirm, rationally, for a sophisticated generation, Christ's teachings of what is the way and the truth and the life.

For one thing—and this is what is lacking in Christianity—Cayce considered a knowledge of the laws of reincarnation and karma to be important for our liberation and our salvation: important in the interests of seeing life clearly and seeing it whole, in the interests of knowing the truth that will set us free, and in the interests of having a proper, intelligent perspective upon this brief and often unintelligible lifetime. "One is what one is," he remarks succinctly in an early reading on reincarnation, "because he was what he was." "Life in its essence is a spiritual force, and it is continuous," he says in another early reading on reincarnation. "And it must, *for the proper understanding, be interpreted as a continuous experience.*"

A passage in the Buddhist scriptures shows us an interesting fragment of conversation between Ananda, one of Buddha's disciples, and Buddha on the subject of karma. "How deep is this causal law!" Ananda

ms. "How deep it seems! . . ." And Buddha answered, saying, "Say
so, Ananda, say not so. Deep indeed is this causal law, and deep it
pears to be. But it is by not knowing, by not understanding, by not
enetrating this doctrine that the world of men has become entangled
like a ball of twine, unable to pass beyond the Way of Woe and the
ceaseless round of rebirth."

Cayce, like Buddha, seems completely persuaded of the fact that *ignorance* of karma and reincarnation can be a hindrance to spiritual
progress, and conversely that *knowledge* of them can be immeasurably
helpful.

Not that a noble and beautiful and fruitful life cannot be lived without this knowledge. Countless men and women of many religious faiths
have lived great and even saintly lives in complete ignorance of, or
disbelief in, reincarnation. And yet it seems likely, to the present writer
at least, that at a certain stage of evolution, a knowledge of reincarnation is indispensable for full comprehension of oneself and of life in
general. The final redemption of self could hardly be made without a
conscious dredging of the past and conscious transmutation of it. Perhaps we have reached the stage of our history where this knowledge is
necessary to us—otherwise it would not be appearing in so many places.

At any rate, the fact that Cayce considered this knowledge important
is clear by obvious inference: had he not thought so, he obviously would
not have, as a therapist, given such information to the troubled people
who came to him for help. It is also clear from many direct quotations
that he did not consider the knowledge of reincarnation to be important merely as an additional piece of intellectual furniture, or the knowledge of one's own karma to be worthwhile merely by way of satisfying
idle curiosity.

"Just to find out that you lived, died, and were buried under a cherry
tree in grandmother's garden," he remarked pointedly in a reading given
in 1937, "does not make you one whit better as a neighbor, citizen, father, or mother. But to know that you spoke unkindly in the past and
suffered for it, and in the present may correct it by being kind—*that* is
worthwhile!"

This sensible comment could well be taken to heart by many people who, becoming convinced of the truth of reincarnation, make eager efforts to discover their own past lives.

At the present time there are two major ways of learning about one's past: (1) reliving or recalling it oneself, through hypnosis, reverie, free association, etc.; or (2) having it told to one by a clairvoyant or a medium.* Both these methods have their advantages and disadvantages, their weaknesses and their strengths. There is, of course, the possibility of error in either of them; there is also the possibility of psychological harm, as well as psychological good. The human mind is capable of both fantasy and deception.

But one very important thing to remember in judging the value and authenticity of any presumable past–life information—no matter how it is obtained—is this: Are there causal sequences apparent in this data that show me how to correct my past errors in the present, or that give me deeper self–understanding?

The costuming of a past–life personality is important, to be sure; a monk's garb will surely have had a different effect upon its wearer than a jester's suit, and will signify a different area of experience; but it is the *psychology* of the personality that is really important. Of what value is it to know that one was a courtesan or a king, a Mississippi river pilot or a peasant in Alsace–Lorraine, a temple dancer in Cambodia or a searcher after California gold, unless one also knows the nucleus of character traits that typified that life and that led to the life complications of the present? Almost anyone can think up grand opera plots of love, treachery, murder, revenge, remorse, sudden death, and all the other human vicissitudes, and identify himself as their hero or villain. But this could be no more than an entertaining exercise in fantasy *unless* there is a psychologically valid relationship shown in terms of moral cause and effect between that past life and the present.

Moreover, none of this is of any real and lasting value unless, in addition to the self–insight gained, there is also the willingness to incor-

---

*Cayce suggests in addition the practice of meditation and the analysis of one's dreams as means of facilitating contact with the superconscious mind and thus ultimately discovering one's previous incarnations.

porate the insight into one's day by day conduct of life. Cayce stressed the conduct of life, in fact, as one major way of freeing oneself from the fetters of karma, past or potential. And this conduct has to do with every department of living: with our ideals, our aims, our thinking, our work, our habits of eating and drinking, our speech, and our treatment of other people. "Not what one was, but what one *does* about what one knows—*that* is what is important!" he said, to someone with excessive and apparently idle curiosity about his former selves.

In fact, Cayce went even further than this and maintained that knowledge, of itself, can be evil. "Knowledge not lived is *sin!*" he exclaimed, more than once. "For remember, knowledge—or the seeking of the tree of knowledge—is the sin. It is the use of what you *do* know for the glory of God that is righteousness."

Knowledge, then, plus the application of knowledge in right conduct, are two important elements in extricating ourselves from the mess we are in. These are of the mind and of the will respectively. We begin to suspect that a third ingredient must be of the soul, or love—and we are right.

Following the emphasis of Christ who said, "These things I command you, that ye love one another," Cayce insisted that love is of the very essence of our redemption from the snares and delusions and sorrows of this world. When he told people to do something "for the glory of God," or "in the name of Christ," or "for the sake of Christ," or "with the Christ consciousness," he was using phrases, all of them, indicative of the substitution of the interests of something *beyond* oneself for one's own self-interest; they are all "mystical" or symbolical ways of putting the notion that we must rise above animal selfishness into the capacity for impersonal love for all created things.

We are back then, curiously enough, to our divine triangle. To win a victory over and liberation from this world, we must put on our strength: the three divine attributes with which we were endowed from the very beginning. With our mind we must seek out the laws of life and death; we must acquire knowledge; we must pursue science. Ignorance and blind faith are unworthy of a man. With our will then we must seek to bring ourselves into intelligent harmony with the laws that we have discovered. But with our soul we must seek to love. . . .

If we wish, we can find interesting parallels between these concepts and the concepts of salvation to be found in Hinduism and Buddhism. Love is to be found, of course, both directly and indirectly, in the Hindu and Buddhist scriptures as well as in the Christian. As a matter of fact, love has in some respects been much more practiced in Hindu and Buddhist countries than in Christian. Buddhists have never in their long history been guilty of such Christian atrocities as an Inquisition, a persecution of "witches," or a religious war; a Society for the Prevention of Cruelty to Animals is unnecessary among the Jains of India, whose ruling principle is *ahimsa*, harmlessness to all living beings, and whose loving concern for all forms of life, including insects, is extraordinary.

But love as a spiritual force and as a principle of human relations is an inherent and paramount part of the Christian teaching;* and gradually, as we have come out of our own barbarism, we have been learning to apply it in more and more areas of our social and psychological thinking.

In any case, it is a curious thing that if we truly love, we find ourselves ultimately in a very similar attitude of soul as that achieved by Hindus and Buddhists in their strivings for liberation. If we have love, we find that we begin to work in the world just as the dedicated Hindu works: for the sake of the beautiful action, and not for the sake of the personal rewards of action. If we do all things, substituting the thought of Christ for the thought of our own ego, we will surely lose that illusory set of ego-attachments that fasten us, in Buddhist persuasion, to the Wheel of Woe and the endless round of births and deaths. We can go on indefinitely, drawing parallels (or seeing subtle differences) among the three faiths.

But once our restless, curious mind is satisfied that mutual confirmations are to be found between the liberation techniques of Christianity and of the two great religions of the East, a greater task lies before us: the task of applying anyone of these methods *today*, in our life—and most especially, perhaps, applying love.

---

*The paramount teaching of the Sufis, in Islamic countries, is also love.

There is a story told about St. Francis, that one day when he was hoeing his garden, someone asked him what he would do if he were to be told that the world would end that night. St. Francis thought for a moment, and then replied, quietly, "I would continue to hoe my garden."

We who live under far more terrible threats of planetary destruction than St. Francis ever dreamed of on the sunny slopes of Italy would do well to ponder his untroubled words. Global wars, hydrogen bombs, natural cataclysms, continental destructions—the mere thought of these things gives many people all over the world a sense of futility and pointlessness in living. But this is not necessary.

No matter what happens in the world outside, I am still custodian, and custodian *only* of my world inside. My thoughts, my emotions, and my behavior are entirely my province. My reactions to good fortune and ill; to war and peace; to deprivation and abundance; to the married or the unmarried state; to being a man or a woman; successful or unsuccessful; beautiful or ugly; the underdog or the overdog; in a dominant race or an oppressed one; in a weak or a strong body; in an inhibited or an uninhibited personality: all these experiences are opportunities, tests, and the material on which I must work to win my salvation. All of us, no doubt, on our long journey pass through all of these pairs of opposites.

These conditions are our ancestral estates. This is our garden. We must set ourselves diligently to hoeing it.

# 20

# Reincarnation: Some Implications for Religion, Art, and Psychology

*On every hand nowadays we hear voiced the presentiment that we are on the verge of* a new age. In almost every field of human endeavor—education, sociology, government, language, architecture, technology—people seem to have the same eager awareness of an impending culture change. We know that atomic energy can transform all our living arrangements; we know too that it is within our power now to recreate the world in the image of universal prosperity and peace.

There is another possibility, to be sure—that of atomic annihilation. . . .

If the Cayce prophetic readings are to be given credence, however, planetary annihilation is not on the immediate agenda of the fates. Cayce *did* indicate that before the end of this century there would be great major changes on the earth's surface. He said that the land would be broken up in the western part of America, part going into the sea; that much of Japan would disappear into the ocean; that the upper

177

portion of Europe would be changed "as in the twinkling of an eye"; that land would appear off the east coast of America; that upheavals in the Arctic and the Antarctic would cause eruptions of volcanoes in the torrid zones; that there would be a shifting of the poles so that frigid and semitropical zones will become more tropical.

How seriously all this should be taken we cannot say. Prophecy was not Edgar Cayce's specialty; many times, when asked about the future, he refused point-blank to answer. Frequently he offered this explanation for his evasiveness: that man's will is free and that he has it within himself, every moment, to create the future. However on some occasions he *did* make positive assertions about the future, and it is interesting that many of these predictions were verified by later events.

For example, on August 29, 1943, he told Colonel Starling in a reading that his biography should be written; that it would be a best seller; that Thomas Sugrue would be an excellent choice as the writer of it; and that the book could be published either as a serial, by *Collier's* magazine, or in book form by Simon and Schuster. Three years later, Thomas Sugrue's book, *Starling of the White House, was* published by Simon and Schuster, and it *did* become a best seller. On May 3, 1946, in fact, it ranked second on the non-fiction best seller lists in forty-six American cities.

As long ago as 1926, Cayce said that the island of Bimini, off the east coast of Florida, was the highest portion left above water of the continent of Atlantis, that an ancient temple could still be found there, "under the slime of ages of sea water," and that the Bimini temple was one of the three places on earth where records of the Atlantean method of temple construction could still be discovered. On April 2, 1956, the *Miami Herald* carried an account of a young man and his father who, in hunting for a buried treasure ship off the coast of Bimini, came across the marble columns of an ancient temple . . . As yet no expedition has followed through on this extraordinary discovery; but it will probably be only a matter of time before full confirmation of the Cayce prediction is forthcoming.

These are only two of many similar examples.

And so, if we are to take Cayce's prophecies with regard to our planet seriously, we can prepare ourselves for drastic upheavals, but definitely not for total extinction. Civilization will go on. And we could well build a superb new global civilization upon the mud and muck of the old.

But there is one important consideration to bear in mind, and that is this: no matter how perfect a new social structure could be, it, too, could only be headed for another Atlantis-like debacle *unless* mankind realizes that there is something more important in life than selfish self-seeking, the gratification of all the body's desires, and even the utopian dream of universal comfort and security. Without some scientifically founded, cosmic philosophy of life, which acknowledges the reality and continuity of the spirit, a new world order—no matter how utopian— could not long resist insidious inner corruption. Aldous Huxley's brilliant novel, *Brave New World,* is an unforgettable demonstration of this very point.

The idea of reincarnation and all it implies of spiritual evolution and purpose in life could well be a concept of pivotal importance for the consummation of a new age that shall be truly enduring and truly illumined.

This principle, actually, is so all-inclusive in its implications for human life that—if it is ever universally accepted—it could not but make a profound change in almost every area of human thinking.

Religion, of course, would be one of the primary areas to be deeply affected. Orthodox Christianity, Judaism, and Mohammedanism do not teach reincarnation; orthodox Buddhism and Hinduism do. Yet all of these groups could be profoundly affected by the reincarnation idea *as substantiated by scientific research.*

The scientific research and substantiation is what is so important. Among Hindus and Buddhists, for example, there is unquestionably a much more long-viewed outlook on life, due to their ingrained belief in many lives; hence a greater tranquillity, perhaps, and a subtler philosophic perspective. There is also much knowledge not known to us.

But at the same time, there are many reincarnationist ideas prevailing among Buddhists and Hindus that are legendary and traditional and that may or may not correspond to the facts. ("If you are rude to your father, you will be born in your next life lame in your right leg; if you are rude to your mother, you will be born lame in your left leg.") The injection of the scientific approach to the subject could liberate these people from much ignorance and superstition and thus lead to a tremendously healthier social outlook.

On the other hand, the scientific substantiation of reincarnation would profoundly affect orthodox Christianity, Judaism, and Mohammedanism— not so much with respect to their essential ethical teachings, perhaps, but with respect to the accessories, theologies, and rituals that have grown up about them.

If we limit our attention only to Christianity, we will see, for example, that the basic and most essential teachings of Christ are *not* destroyed, but rather substantiated by reincarnation and karma: namely, love your brother and love the Lord; do unto others as you would have others do unto you. But theological accessories such as baptism, heaven–hell concepts, resurrection, salvation, etc., to which so many orthodox groups cling so tenaciously and so separatively, with so much hostility as regards differing interpretations, will be seen to be, (1) far less important than their proponents believe, and (2) much in need of reevaluation on a symbolic rather than a literal level.

Moreover, much of the guilt that torments people because of the irrational nature of Christian theology (notably the doctrine of "original sin"), and many of the complexes and schizophrenic conflicts arising from the irreconcilable disparity between science and theological dogma would disappear if the rational, logical, and cosmic psychology of reincarnation won universal acceptance.

Matters concerning the soul and the afterlife have long been regarded as the exclusive property of priests and Holy Books, and men have been expected to give them blind unreasoning faith. But with the application of the scientific method to these areas, we can finally see the possibility of a world view in religion rather than many tribal views, each one bigoted and blind, in its way, and separated the one from the other largely because of semantic confusions.

We do not have one algebra in England and a different algebra in Brazil; algebra is algebra, the world over, and so is physics and chemistry. Why? Because the scientific method usually arrives at the same conclusions. Research in the religious field could similarly lead to universality among men.

The arts constitute another field of human activity that could be deeply affected by the reincarnation view.

There has been for a long time in the Western world a growing sense of exhaustion and repetitiousness with regard to art. The destruction of many of the art treasures of Europe during World War II was conventionally lamented by the press, but regarded with a sense of relief, either frank or concealed, on the part of many artists. This relief was occasioned by the sense that there is nothing new to be said or done in art. The old tradition has exhausted itself, and though various attempts at a new tradition have appeared in all the arts, they have no central unitary world view or world idea, acceptable alike to science and sentiment, and of sufficiently universal validity to have any great creative force or integrative power. The Christian point of view, so long the fountainhead of Western art, has unmistakably lost its impetus and its power to inspire anything of artistic significance.

The reincarnation principle, and all the ancient wisdom of which it is a part, could now step forward to supply the necessary unifying concept. The realization that man has a cosmic meaning and purpose could vitalize the currents of man's thinking about himself and his destiny. It would also inevitably inspire him to the creation of new art forms and to the utterance of things not yet said in the modern world.

The vastness of this new outlook needs the ordering hand of the artist so that man will not feel afraid in the new, systematic but strange immensity that surrounds him. He must learn to feel at home in the universe, and in the solar system which is his school and playground. The great cycles of development, the rhythmic alternations between earth and other-plane expression, the tremendous evolutionary spans, the colossal yet minute justice of the power of karma, the infinitely gradated stages on the path of evolutionary unfoldment, the complexity of interrelationships between incarnations, individuals, bodily vehicles—all these new concepts need to be sensed and understood by the artist, and then compressed, simplified, framed, reduced to understandable terms so that other men will be reassured and activated on new levels of energy.

It is highly probable that there would be a mathematical trend in this new artistic utterance. It is probable because the universe itself is mathematical and man's destiny is in so many respects mathematically conditioned. Cycles have a periodicity that is numerically measurable. All sounds and colors have their distinct wave lengths and vibratory rate. Man himself, together with all his organs and mental activities, is, we are told, of certain distinct vibrations. Delicate, mathematical exactitude fused with creative fancy on cosmic themes would undoubtedly form a definite genre of future art, should reincarnation and karma win universal acceptance. It is already found in the works of Claude Bragdon and of that little known genius, Hubert Stowitts.

Painting, of course, would to a high degree lend itself to the art expression of an illumined age. As clairvoyant research reveals more and more of the worlds of subtler reality that surround us, the artist will find himself with an embarrassment of riches as far as subject matter is concerned. The pictorial representation of successive incarnations is only one of many possibilities. At first this could be done imaginatively or impressionistically; later it could, with clairvoyant gifts or clairvoyant collaboration, be done with more biographical precision.

In the period of psychological and religious adjustment that may well need to take place if reincarnation is incontrovertibly proved in our laboratories, the literary artist will have a highly important service to perform. To the orthodox, to the uncertain, to the skeptical, to the bewildered people of our time, the writer must give reassurance and insight. He will be, as writers always are, the midwife to the birth pangs of the new era. He must translate into human terms a teaching that is supremely human, but difficult of comprehension to people schooled in the psychologically unrealistic teachings of Christian orthodoxy.

By no means would all fiction of the future need to be ponderous with psychological and cosmic issues, however. On the contrary. The comedy of life's conjunctions is fully as real as their tragedy. Indeed, with this more Olympian point of vantage we could view the antics of men with the same perspective that through all the centuries has made the hills reverberate with the laughter of the gods.

The comic possibilities of character delineation are infinitely enlarged by the contrasts observable from life to life and relationship to relationship. Dramatic irony could take on a more piquant and scientific character as one observes the alteration of role and station that takes place from one life to the next.

By the throwing open of all the halls of destiny, wit, too, would be given an inexhaustible playground of paradox and fantasy. As we contemplate the new mansions wherein man, the monarch and midget, finds himself housed, we cannot but find exquisitely ridiculous elements in the new-found but uncertain dignity with which he finds himself invested.

Indeed, a whole new undertone of joyousness could pervade the literature of the future, for it would have been freed from the miasmic unhealthy swamps of Freudianism and the deadening irreality of materialism. The merriment of nations would increase rather than otherwise, if men learn that their tragedies are only temporary stations on a pathway leading to liberation.

But it is perhaps in the area of psychology that the most immediate and drastic transformation could take place.

The reincarnation principle, in opening up the tremendously deep stretches of the unconscious, can give us a far more rational explanation of life's difficulties than can any other system of thought. In reminding us that we are essentially spirits rather than animals, and that our goal is not merely survival but perfection and expansion of consciousness, the reincarnation principle makes possible a new purposiveness. And in showing us how the laws of karma inexorably operate, a new sense of the ethical validity of religious precepts becomes crystal clear.

Thus the reincarnation principle gives us explanation, purposiveness, and ethics in life; scientifically validated, it can bring about a union of science, medicine, philosophy, psychology, ethics, and religion—a consummation, surely, devoutly to be wished.

We have already speculated on the effects that the reincarnation idea could have in the field of art. Not only would it affect the subject matter and the treatment of art, infusing it with a new unitary world view, but also it could infuse each one of us with the awareness that it is the destiny of each of us to become creative artists ourselves.

Ahead of us is the prospect of perfection and genius, in any and all creative fields. But beauty is as much the aim of mankind as genius or creative power. Genius is insight and creative power with respect to the *not-self*—the objects, shapes, colors, lines, materials, textures of the outer world. Personal beauty is insight and creative power with respect to the *self*. All of us must strive to achieve mastery both with respect to the not-self and the self.

The male tends to be centrifugal, or out-looking; the female tends to be centripetal, or in-looking; so perhaps it can be said that genius is more typically the male ideal, and beauty more typically the female. But inasmuch as both sexes are at present merely specializations, separated halves of the one androgynous being, all of us, regardless of our present sex, must finally achieve both genius and beauty.

Where does a person lack creative power? Where does he lack beauty? Where does he lack balance? These are important questions for the therapist to ask—far more important in a way than what was his toilet training as a child and did he hate his father. The latter questions may have significance too, to be sure; but we must learn to look up as well as down, forward as well as backward; we must learn to contemplate the archetypal goal as much as the animal prototype.

With the new knowledge of reincarnation and with the other great supersensory potentials of man, our planet could finally come out of the dark ages it has been enshrouded in for so long. It may be that this sad world—so aptly called by Bernard Shaw the "lunatic asylum of the solar system"—will at last become what it can be: a luminous place, filled with men and women who have not only become acquainted with their evil and befuddled past, but have also learned how to transform it and transmute it into a thing of light and of beauty.

# Index

## DISCOVER HOW THE EDGAR CAYCE MATERIAL CAN HELP YOU!

The Association for Research and Enlightenment, Inc. (A.R.E.®), was founded in 1931 by Edgar Cayce. Its international headquarters are in Virginia Beach, Virginia, where thousands of visitors come year-round. Many more are helped and inspired by A.R.E.'s local activities in their own hometowns or by contact via mail (and now the Internet!) with A.R.E. headquarters.

People from all walks of life, all around the world, have discovered meaningful and life-transforming insights in the A.R.E. programs and materials, which focus on such areas as personal spirituality, holistic health, dreams, family life, finding your best vocation, reincarnation, ESP, meditation, and soul growth in small-group settings. Call us today at our toll-free number:

### 1-800-333-4499

or

Explore our electronic visitors center on the
Internet: **http://www.edgarcayce.org.**

We'll be happy to tell you more about how the work of the A.R.E. can help you!

A.R.E.
215 67th Street
Virginia Beach, VA 23451-2061